ELEMENTARY SCHOOL
CAREERS EDUCATION

A Humanistic Model

THE MERRILL SERIES
IN CAREER PROGRAMS

ELEMENTARY SCHOOL CAREERS EDUCATION

A Humanistic Model

FRANK R. CROSS
Oregon State University

CHARLES E. MERRILL PUBLISHING COMPANY
A Bell & Howell Company
Columbus, Ohio

Published by
Charles E. Merrill Publishing Company
A Bell & Howell Company
Columbus, Ohio 43216

Library of Congress Catalog Card Number: 73-92002

ISBN: 0-675-08824-0

1 2 3 4 5 6—78 77 76 75 74

Printed in the United States of America

TO
MARIE

THE MERRILL SERIES IN CAREER PROGRAMS

In recent years our nation has literally redis-covered education. Concurrently, many nations are considering educational programs in revolutionary terms. They now realize that education is the responsible link between social needs and social improvement. While traditionally Americans have been committed to the ideal of the optimal development of each individual, there is increased public appreciation and support of the values and benefits of education in general, and vocational and technical education in particular. With occupational education's demonstrated capacity to contribute to economic growth and national well being, it is only natural that it has been given increased prominence and importance in this educational climate.

With the increased recognition that the true resources of a nation are its human resources, occupational education programs are considered a form of investment in human capital—an investment which provides comparatively high returns to both the individual and society.

The Merrill Series in Career Programs is designed to provide a broad range of educational materials to assist members of the profession in providing effective and efficient programs of occupational education which contribute to an individual's becoming both a contributing economic producer and a responsible member of society.

The series and its sub-series do not have a singular position or philosophy concerning the problems and alternatives in providing the broad range of offerings needed to prepare the nation's work force. Rather, authors are encouraged to develop and support independent positions and alternative strategies. A wide range of educational and occupational experiences and perspectives have been brought to bear through the Merrill Series in Career Programs National Editorial Board. These experiences, coupled with those of the authors, assure useful publications. I believe that this title, along with others in the series, will provide major assistance in further developing and extending viable educational programs to assist youth and adults in preparing for and furthering their careers.

Robert E. Taylor
Editorial Director
Series in Career Programs

PREFACE

This book is an attempt to construct an educational model that combines the intent of career education with the strengths of elementary education. The intent of the book is (1) to provide a point of departure for designing elementary careers education programs; (2) to encourage dialogue about the mission and method of elementary education among in-service and students preparing to teach; and (3) to elicit more questions than answers, irritate more than soothe, and inspire new visions of children learning rather than perpetuate old ones.

This is more a book of ideals than a book of ideas.

Ideals should precede ideas. Ideals breathe life into ideas and give them vitality. When ideas that are not the offspring of ideals are given instructional importance in the schools, children can and do suffer the consequences of an irrelevant education.

Our way of life is based on certain human ideals. To deny their importance in designing educational programs is to deny children educational contacts with the heart and soul of their cultural heritage. To exclude these ideals from the goals of the schools is to threaten our very existence. To include them is to grant our children a chance at survival in a world in which human fulfillment can be a reality for all people, regardless of race, religion, or socioeconomic status. The model of elementary education proposed in this book is dedicated to these ideals and their achievement.

This book was inspired more by the needs of children than by the desires of adults.

Schools are for children and at the very least they should be ideal places in which to spend part of childhood. The educational model proposed in this book offers opportunities for program designers and teachers to take advantage of what is known about how children develop and learn. It is flexible enough to permit them to extend their uniqueness in many experimental and exploratory directions.

This book is intended to be a vision of what can be rather than a statement of what is.

Most of the visions we have of teaching and classrooms are centered around schools as they have existed over an extended period of time. If education is to emerge into an experience that is more attuned to the times and more humane in its treatment of children, educational programs and practices will need to reflect new visions of quality school living and how to achieve it.

This book is an uncomplicated description of a complex proposal.

When teachers read professional literature, their thought processes should translate the author's thoughts into their own images of how to advance the living and learning of children. Teaching and learning are complex processes that should not be further complicated by a language or writing style that frustrates communication, "turns off" both educators and patrons, and prevents sound ideals and ideas from ever reaching the classroom. The pressure of semantic interpretation has been relaxed here in an effort to assist teachers and students who are preparing to teach to envision a better education for children than now generally exists.

This book is a guide rather than a set of specifications.

No printed statement can solve local education problems or "plug the holes" found in teacher education programs. Only people can do this. Put to its best use, this book can be a source of ideals and ideas, encourage the beginnings of change, and serve as a basis for examining existing educational effort. It is a statement of genuine concern for the education of American boys and girls. It is offered for whatever value and use it may have in bringing to our children an educational experience worthy of their humanness.

The organization of the book is absent of mystic intent. The chapters are arranged in what seems to be a logical order for unveiling and explaining the elementary school careers education model. Chapter 1 offers a rationale for the emergence of career education and a discussion of definitions of career education at the national, state, and local levels and by individual writers. Chapter 2 presents and discusses the three-dimensional model of elementary school career education upon which the book is based. The first dimension of the model, living, is the focus of Chapter 3. More emphasis is placed on the "living" dimension because generally it has not been included in other literature. Chapter 4 covers the other two dimensions, learning and curricular areas, and deals briefly with the permeating influences (aesthetics, spiritual and moral values, and physical development). Chapter 5 considers personnel preparation and renewal, and factors of achieving program success. Chapter 6 closes the book with consideration of organization and use of community resources.

Acknowledgment must be given to the many national, state, and local educators who have generously made their ideas and printed materials available to all who were interested enough to ask. Gratitude is expressed to a group of Oregon elementary school principals who were an invaluable source of ideas and inspiration. Special recognition is given to Marie Cross, my wife, for her many hours of work on the manuscript, and her efforts to keep this an honest and readable statement of human concern.

CONTENTS

ELEMENTARY SCHOOL CAREERS EDUCATION

A Humanistic Model

Chapter 1 RATIONALE FOR CHANGE

Introduction

Career education has been heralded by many of its proponents as the means of resolving the multitude of problems confronting our nation and professional education. Career education in and of itself is capable of solving very few problems. As a vehicle of change, it can be the means of bringing to education a new excitement and a new direction that could result in a more relevant experience for all learners and bring to our people a more satisfying and productive way of life. It can provide them with the means for dealing successfully with the social, technological, and environmental conditions that threaten our biological and national survival.

Education has only that value which is evidenced by the performance of its product. It can influence the lives of individuals and nations only by aiding its clients in acquiring the attitudes, knowledge, and skills needed to meet the demands of current living and face confidently an unknown future. It cannot be antiquated in its goals or myopic in its view of the future. Neither can education ignore the fact that its raw material is human, nor that its outcomes must be concerned with improving the quality of human living for all; regardless of origin, religion, socioeconomic condition, or occupation. Educators must not be permitted to forget that survival

1

depends upon how well they provide for the preservation and advancement of desirable human qualities.

This nation was founded by men and women who dared to imagine a better world in which to live. It was made great by dreamers who had the imagination, the courage, and the drive to make their visions real. What may be needed at this crucial time in our nation's history is an entire generation of dreamers who not only envision a more beautiful and satisfying world in which to raise their children and find fulfillment, but who possess, in addition to courage, imagination and drive, the values, skills, and knowledge necessary to achieve human goals in a technological society. If we are to survive in a humanly acceptable condition focused upon quality living, we must build upon the dreams of youth and not let them fade into oblivion on taking a family, assuming adult civic responsibilities, or entering the world of work. "A man's destiny often lies buried in the images of his youth . . . before greatness comes the image of greatness" (22:23).

The preservation of youthful aspirations requires an education that builds upon the goals of learners and helps them discover how to perfect their immediate society in a way that is transferable to their adult lives. The process of education should maintain the uninhibited, creative, and curious character of the young and, at least in part, commute for adults the sentence of being denied participation in the excitement of learning that is so much a part of childhood. Concurrent with making learning an exciting and necessary part of living, the educational system must provide for the continuous growth of young learners toward independent thought and responsible action.

Rationale for Change

We must match our concern for preserving the positive characteristics of youth as they move toward responsible adult living with an educational program capable of meeting such a challenge. Responsible educators need to develop and implement new programs capable of allaying current unhappiness over the quality of education received by our children. The historic educational objectives of self-realization, human relationship, economic efficiency, and civic responsibility should not be permitted to maintain their aloofness in the midst of this war of verbal and literary condemnation of daily happenings in the classroom.

The teaching profession must direct its efforts to rebuilding lost patronage for it appears from the abundance of criticism that it has generated only negative feelings among its clients and patrons. Within the profession, both prince and pauper have contributed to the public attitude through damning publications and biting verbal barrages. As a result, we are being told that, unless dramatic improvements are implemented soon, public education as we know it could and should disappear from the American scene. Parents may band together to provide a new breed of private school; school boards may contract for the instruction of children in their districts with companies that are at this moment developing "packaged" instructional programs for general consumption; various forms of mass media may offer listeners, readers, and viewers instruction in a great variety of areas and in ways that have greater sensory appeal to the learner than the usual school approaches. Such programs can hardly provide the total education required to face successfully and happily the future prophesied by our landings on the moon and the concern our young have for conquering human sufferings.

Critical evaluation must precede significant change and any profession, if it is in fact a profession, should welcome well-intended criticism of its performance, but the problem in education is that the criticism is as incomplete as education is said to be. Few have given intellectual dignity to their fault-finding by offering alternatives to the educational programs they choose to criticize. Many sincere and dedicated educators find themselves living in a perpetual state of frustration because of the obvious incompatibility between what is currently taking place in the name of education and their interpretation of what is real and important in today's world of unrest and uncertainty. Their investigations have led them to believe that little of what is going on in our contemporary schools can be justified in human terms. What they need is more viable and relevant alternatives than have been available in the past or have been offered by critics.

We are told that if current educational performance is the best we have to offer, schools cannot continue to remain open and expect the continued support of the public. Public trust demands that the product of education be generations of people who are sensitive to and concerned about other humans, and who are aware of their relationship to the environment. Survival will depend upon how honestly and completely people internalize the feeling that life in all its forms has value and importance. Such a commitment must become a prime outcome of education.

To meet this basic requirement of continued existence, individuals must be capable of continuous learning, skilled in the multiplicities of problem solving and decision making, possessors of a positive self-concept, and accepting of all humans as worthy and equal. Chasnoff stated that society wants to produce people with the following qualities:

1. Individuals whose healthy sense of personal autonomy and social empathy are reflected in mature personal, social, and political behavior.
2. Innovators ready to use their knowledge to devise ways to help rather than exploit others.
3. Citizens creative enough to invent, support, and insure peaceful political methods and productive, satisfying lives for all people. (2:2)

These objectives are basic to facing and solving the mysteries of life in an unknown future and must become significant outcomes of education.

New programs that offer greater hope of achieving the goals of education need to be designed and implemented through processes of change that ensure more effective results than have been realized to date. Most of the attempts made toward educational change have done little more than rearrange the factors of learning on the surface while the nature of the instruction going on behind the classroom door continued unabated and unchanged. Resurrected educators of the 1850s could find sanctuary from the awesome technological advances of this age by seeking asylum in what to them would be the familiar surroundings of many modern-day classrooms.

Somehow we must find the means of shedding the skin we long ago outgrew. The conditions of our educational past and the assumptions we conjured up to justify them must be relegated to their rightful place in history, and we must now move into a more enlightened era in which we base our educational thinking and programs on the known needs of children and society. There can be no professional survival if we continue to do what is wrong or inappropriate, or both, when there is so much we know how to do well.

There are those who would argue for the demise of public education on the grounds that the new technology can provide programs more capable of keeping abreast with the rapid expansion of knowledge than those programs now available in our public schools. This argument would be difficult to rebut if remaining even with the knowledge explosion is all there is to educating our offspring. Education is more than that—much more! Education is the difference between surviving in some psycho-mechanistic form and surviving as decent human beings with compassion for other "naked apes." If this is an accurate assessment of what education should be, then all we know about the human as a learning individual, as an affective being, and as a social entity must become an important foundation upon which to build the skills of living, and it is within the life careers that these qualities of life can be most effectively developed.

Career Education

Emerging from this discontent and disaffection for public education on the part of the paying public and from the uncertainty and frustration of educators, is a program with the professed attributes of being able to reunite education and its patrons in a more relevant, productive, and compatible union. Career education has emerged at this point in educational history primarily because of factors and pressures outside the profession. For the first time, change in education is being defined and initiated by forces outside educational circles. Reasons for this emergence are undoubtedly many and as yet not totally identifiable, but Reinhart has identified five reasons for public demand and acceptance for career education:

> The political realities which undergird the emerging careers curriculum are the result of a convergence of social and economic phenomena. . . . As long as America's public schools ignore their vocational responsibility to *all* men and *all* work, they will be in trouble with the public.
>
> Second, the quality of the nation's educational system is now being measured in terms of national survival. . . . As long as educational inadequacies limit our response to totalitarianism and economic dominance abroad, many citizens and officials will continue to feel that our dysfunctional schools are enormously detrimental, that conceivably they may cost our freedom or even our lives.
>
> Third, the continued increase in poverty and its ascending social and economic costs drain the reservoir of resources for attaining national goals. . . . The continued allocation of Federal dollars to drain the problem of the pool of unemployed, without giving attention to reducing the flow into the pool, is wasteful and inefficient. As long as American education is conceived as contributing to the flow, it will be expected to reform itself.
>
> Fourth, the civil rights movement that erupted in the sixties has drawn dramatic attention to the social, economic, and political deprivations borne by the nation's minorities. . . . As increasing numbers of minority group members "come of age" politically, public education will be forced to respond to their distinct needs.
>
> Finally, a general disenchantment with the educational system in America has tended to accentuate the community concern about public education and stimulate the expression of the layman's point of view. . . . Since public opinion is generally supportive of career education, increased disaffection with the public school system will tend to increase the public demand for a careers curriculum. (18:1–2)

There is agreement that education must change and there appears to be agreement among the public that career education is an acceptable and logical direction in which to go. There is much less agreement, even among educators, as to what career education is all about. A generally accepted definition has not emerged and it may be pedagogically wrong to expect one because there appears to be more than one philosophical base upon which career education is being designed.

DEFINITIONS OF CAREER EDUCATION

The mention of career education seems to conjure up visions of students sawing boards and pounding nails rather than engaging in the "important activities" of learning. Many make an instant interpretation of career education as being no more than a crafty new name for vocational education and consequently no more acceptable than it was in its old trappings. Because of the "dumping ground" view held by many nonvocational educators and lay people, there is an unwillingness to accept any program that is suspected of vocational leanings. In order to overcome this, definitions will have to be stated so that even the narrowest-minded reader will clearly understand the new benefits learners can derive from the proposed program. According to Marland this defining will have to take place at the operational level:

> *Career education cannot be defined solely in Washington. Revolution doesn't happen because government suggests it. We can ask many of the questions, we can help with funds, but if career education is to be the revolutionary instrument that the times demand it will be defined in hard and urgent debate across the land by teachers, laymen, students, and administrators in months to come. Let that debate start now.* (21:10)

Defining career education at the operational level will require that educators reach agreement with their communities concerning the functions of schools in our culture. In part this decision must be concerned with whether education should be a leader or a follower in effecting social change. It must be decided whether career education is to be the means of perpetuating an industrial and materialistic society or whether there are current conditions that require a reassessment of values and the establishment of new directions. Until all such issues are resolved, workable decisions cannot be made relative to the definition of career education.

At present, definitions of career education can be placed on a continuum that has vocational education at one extreme and "life careers" education at the other. Definitions find their position on the continuum in terms of the expressed relationship between the vocational career and other education. Everyone agrees that the vocational career has great importance to any career education program, but there is little agreement as to whether that importance is one of *supremacy, centrality,* or *equality.*

A program that gives *supremacy* to the vocational component is based on the philosophical position that the conditions of life are and should be determined by vocational membership. It assumes that the quality of life can be improved by maximally preparing for an occupation or profession that has been matched carefully to the capabilities and interests of the individual. Such a position supports an educational program that directs its total energies to achieving these vocational goals. *Centrality* of importance places the vocational component in a position of being a central theme around which other components are organized. It suggests that an individual's vocation has greater influence on life style than other components, but it in turn is influenced by other factors of living. In the educational setting, this position results in organizing the program in a way that relates all learning to vocational aspects of the program and in a manner that permits the vocational emphasis to give relevance and practicality to all other educational experiences. A position of *equality* exists when more than one life career is associated with total life style and each career is dependent upon and influenced by the others. Quality of living is determined by success in each career and by the individual's ability to integrate them into a fulfilling life style. An educational program based upon a "life careers" model would be developed around experiences appropriate to helping individuals achieve successful performance in each of the life roles.

Whether it is possible to determine a school's philosophy of education by examining its definition of career education is doubtful, but there should be some positive relationship between what is believed and what is advocated. With this in mind, the following discussion is not intended to be an analytical exercise directed at identification of philosophical position but rather a means of providing an opportunity for readers to test a variety of working definitions of career education against their personal philosophies of education, and to acquaint them with a limited sample of definitions generated at the national, state, and local level and by individuals writing and working in the field of career education.

NATIONAL LEVEL

Much of the activity in career education is taking place at the national level. The U. S. Office of Education under the leadership of Commissioner Marland has made career education its main area of emphasis and has influenced greatly definitions of career education. Marland views career education as "cradle-to-grave" learning with the public schools assuming responsibility for providing experiences designed to orient young children into the world of work, permit them to explore vocational possibilities in the middle grades, and during the later years of public school develop entry level skills for a specific occupation or for further formal education. His position was reported as follows in *College and University Business:*

> As Marland tentatively envisions it, the reshaping of education would take the form of an inverted pyramid. Attitude building, career orientation, vocational guidance, as well as exploratory activities, would begin in the elementary grades to create motivation for a world of work. Specific skill exploration would start in the middle grades to acquaint students with machines, instruments, tools, and equipment. Simple job cluster skills would be introduced in junior high school. As the student progressed through secondary and post secondary programs of his choice, he would have alternative choices for specific skills training, for job cluster skills training, for prevocational and pretechnical education, for advanced voca-

tional and technical education, and for college preparatory education. Upgrading and retraining through continued education programs would also exist through adulthood. (14:40)

At the Ohio State University the U. S. Office of Education sponsored the development of a Comprehensive Career Education Model that has been accepted as a pilot program in six educational settings: Hackensack, New Jersey; Pontiac, Michigan; Jefferson County, Colorado; Atlanta, Georgia; Mesa, Arizona; and Los Angeles, California. The school-based Comprehensive Career Education Model was developed around the following tenets:

1. Career education is a comprehensive educational program focused on careers. It begins with the entry of the child into a formal school program and continues into the adult years.
2. Career education involves all students, regardless of their post-secondary plans.
3. Career education involves the entire school program and the resources of the community.
4. Career education infuses the total school curriculum, rather than providing discrete, high-profile "career education" blocks forced into the curriculum.
5. Career education unites the students, his parents, the schools, the community, and employers in a cooperative educational adventure.
6. Career education provides the student with information and experiences representing the entire world of work.
7. Career education supports the student from initial career awareness, to career exploration, careers direction-setting, career preparation and career placement, and provides for placement follow-through including re-education if desired.
8. Career education is not a synonym for vocational education; but, vocational preparation is an integral and important part of a total career education system. (15:16)

Also at the national level, the National Association of State Directors of Vocational Education has identified, in a *Position Paper on Career Education,* a set of career education characteristics that are similar to the tenets of the school-based Comprehensive Career Education Model. In their paper, it took the following position:

> In the quest for relevancy in education, nothing is more pertinent than providing every youth with the capability to make intelligent career decisions—and the opportunity to prepare for entry and progress in such careers.
> Central to the belief that career decisions must be made through sensible choice rather than by hap-hazard change—and that actual preparation for entry into careers in an organized, purposeful manner is a self-evident

requisite—is the proposition that public education, from kindergarten through college, must set about making arrangements of organization and instruction that will meet such needs.

It is this latter component of Career Education—that of opportunity to prepare for employment—which can be well-served by contemporary programs of occupational education. To deny this climaxing opportunity . . . is to nullify the purpose of Career Education and is to make futile a realistic goal of education.

In this context, we believe further that the following characteristics are inherent and essential aspects of Career Education:

1. Career education is not synonymous with vocational education but vocational education is a major part of career education.
2. Career education enhances rather than supplants public school educational programs.
3. Career education is an integral part of the present structure of the public schools.
4. Career education involves all students—and all educators.
5. Career education involves extensive orientation and exploration of occupational opportunities.
6. Career education emphasizes individual instruction and student determination.
7. Career education is a continuum that begins at kindergarten and extends throughout employment.
8. Career education contributes to student incentive and aspirations.
9. Career education includes specific preparation for occupations.
10. Career education assures realistic occupational choice.
11. Career education promotes wholesome attitudes toward all useful work.
12. Career education permits each student to realistically assess personal attributes as a part of setting life goals.
13. Career education provides a means of articulation from grade to grade and level to level. (16:1–2)

National professional education organizations, other than vocational education organizations, have not at this time made known their position relative to career education. If these organizations lend their assistance and prestige to the movement, the attempt to improve the human conditions and regain lost professional dignity may be successful. It is no compliment to these organizations that much of the growth and acceptance of career education has been inspired to a large degree from outside the profession. When the public expresses general unhappiness with current education and indicates an interest in the objectives of career education, it would seem appropriate for national organizations to be the first to react and develop a statement of position. Definitions of career education are not currently available from this national source.

STATE LEVEL

There is career education activity in each of the fifty states. Some of this activity is limited to isolated projects funded from the national level. In a few states an effort is being made to initiate career education in every school system. Some state departments of education have shown little interest, while others have directed a substantial portion of available resources to the design and implementation of career education programs. Some states are just awakening to the arrival of career education on the scene, whereas a number of states are highly involved in effecting its arrival. It would be impossible, and unnecessary, to report the position each state has taken; but it is necessary and valuable to present a general overview of state-level definitions.

The availability of published career education material, as well as the quantity and descriptive quality of publications, varies greatly from state to state. Several states have not as yet published materials. In others all efforts are being directed at providing human or budgetary resources to local-level programs rather than at producing materials. In several states, uncomplicated statements of intent are currently all that are available. A few state departments of education are extensively involved in publishing materials and in providing other kinds of resources.

The only criteria followed in selecting the programs reported here were that the specific state was doing something and the materials were at hand and reportable.

Oregon.   A massive effort is underway in Oregon to make career education a reality in all school districts and at all levels—kindergarten through college. The Oregon Board of Education and the School of Education at Oregon State University have worked closely together to achieve the state's goal of implementing career education at all levels by 1975. The Division of Career Education of the Oregon Board of Education has published a set of proposed accomplishments and a list of objectives that define the nature of the state's career education program:

Proposed Accomplishments
1. Assuring that all instruction is relevant to the real life concerns of students so that they develop the basic skills, knowledges, and values that will be essential for success in any career they might choose.
2. Providing all with ample opportunities to explore the knowledge, skills, technical requirements, working conditions, and political and social environments and responsibilities of each of the career fields that are open to them.

3. Providing guidance services adequate to assure that every young person gains expert help in assessing his personal interests, aptitudes and abilities, in making career choices, and in planning an appropriate educational program.

4. Providing a high school curriculum based on career goals that will allow all students to prepare for the occupational fields of their choice by acquiring skills and knowledges that will enable them to (a) obtain entry-level employment in jobs not requiring advanced training, and (b) continue education and training in post-high school institutions or in business and industry.

5. Assuring that opportunities for advanced occupational preparations are readily accessible to all persons through community colleges, other public and private post-high school programs or business and industry. (12: not numbered)

Objectives:

1. Enhance learning about careers at the elementary school level in order to enlarge a child's understanding of vocational choice and develop economic competence in a changing world of work.

2. Provide for concurrent planning, program expansion, and identification of supportive exploratory occupational programs, grades 7 through 10.

3. Provide for articulation and coordination of the efforts of all educational agencies, secondary and post-secondary, so that all clientele served may benefit from uninterrupted instructional sequences.

4. Redefine the role of occupational education in the public schools to assume a major role in the field of man power development (training people to work).

5. Develop and implement occupational guidance and counseling programs to be continuing integral parts of the educational program provided all students in the public school system.

6. Adopt specific programs to develop employability in every student and work with agencies to bring about placement.

7. Develop and implement (in cooperation with other public and private agencies) regular vocational technical programs which will serve disadvantaged and handicapped persons. Also, plan and initiate special job training programs to serve those persons who cannot succeed in regular vocational technical programs. (13:2–3)

South Carolina. The Exemplary Project in Career Education in South Carolina, Region V, was initiated in 1970 under Part D of Public Law 90–576. The program is composed of five components: Elementary Career Orientation, Work Experience, Vocational Interdisciplinary Program, Intensive Training, and Placement and Follow-up, and is defined as an effort to:

... stimulate the development in South Carolina School Districts of specific activities and programs in career education which are designed to

assist students in clarifying self-identity, developing good attitudes expanding career knowledge and job skills leading to appropriate job placement and/or continuing education. . . . (20:7)

The South Carolina Project is based on the requirements of the Office of
Education program guidelines for Part D—Exemplary Program section of
the 1968 Vocational Education Amendments which state that participating
schools will make provisions for:

1. Broad occupational orientation at the elementary and secondary levels
   so as to increase student awareness of the range of options open to them
   in the world of work.
2. Work experience, cooperative education and similar programs, making
   possible a wide variety of offerings in many occupational areas.
3. Activities designed to develop and broaden curricular offerings.
4. Students not previously enrolled in vocational programs to receive
   specific training in job entry skills just prior to the time that they leave
   the school.
5. Intensive occupational guidance and counseling during the last years
   of school and for initial placement of all students at the completion of
   their schooling. (20:7)

New Jersey.   The program in New Jersey, entitled "Technology for
Children," was initiated before the current excitement for career education
entered upon the educational scene and undoubtedly influenced some of the
early thinking in career education. "Technology for Children" (T4C) is
designed to employ direct "hands-on" learning experiences from the world
of technology as the means of achieving instructional objectives. It is intended to give children a modern curriculum; one that deals with the reality
of living in our technological society rather than meeting the conditions set
by conceptual objectives established in another time.

There appears to be no one statement defining "Technology for Children." The T4C program has been widely publicized and excerpts from
those writings give a general, if incomplete, view of the intent of the program. Elliot agreed that T4C is not easy to define:

T4C is not one of those programs that is easily described in a single,
succinct statement.

T4C is not really another kind of occupational orientation, although the
world of work permeates the entire program.

And T4C is not really vocational education in the familiar sense of the
word.

The broad theory behind T4C is that there's no getting away from our
world of technology—especially for children who will enter a world that
is even more highly technological than it is today.

What this means in practice is that children in the T4C program learn language arts, sciences, mathematics and social studies by making things. (5:64)

Idaho. "Guidelines for a Comprehensive Educational Program" have been prepared by the State Department of Education and the State Department of Vocational Education in Idaho. Career education is seen as a part of comprehensive education and not as an appendage to an existing program. The Comprehensive Educational Program is described as a three-dimensional model constructed around Functions, Levels and Focus. The identified functions of education are: intellectual, physical, social, and personal. Levels of education are the usual organizational levels: pre-school, elementary, secondary, post-secondary and adult. Awareness, exploration, experimentation, preparation, and application are the subcategories listed under focus and education. Career education is defined in terms of the model:

> Career education combines the academic world and the world of work. It must be a part of the education program at all levels from kindergarten through the university and life. A complete program of Career Education includes awareness of the world of work, broad exploration of occupations, in-depth exploration of selected clusters, and career preparation for all students, either in the secondary school, the four-year college, post secondary vocational-technical school, or in other education programs. To accomplish this the basic educational subjects should incorporate Career Education as a major activity throughout the curriculum. (11:2–3)

The stated goals of the Idaho program are:

> *Learning to Live*—means developing a self-awareness of one's capabilities and developing the ability to utilize leisure time and understand society in general.
> *Learning to Learn*—involves the motivation of students by making education subjects meaningful and relevant to life and the world of work.
> *Learning to Make a Living*—means preparing students with the capability to support themselves economically and to become productive members of the community. (11:2–3)

Pennsylvania. The Pennsylvania Department of Education is in the process of developing a state plan for career education for implementation in the near future. Four model projects have been supported from the state level. Materials and procedures employed in these projects are to be replicated and packaged for use in interested school districts in the state. Legislation has been written that would establish a Career Education Commission to oversee the Department of Education's career education efforts, thereby providing necessary legislative support. The following statements were taken from a document on career education prepared and published in the Pennsylvania Department of Education Office:

> Career education is the blending of the academic with the vocational in the process of educating all persons during their entire lives to be aware of the variety of opportunities for work that exist in their community and in the nation. It prepares the individuals by establishing foundations for their working lives based upon identified interests and talents to the end that they will be able to make effective use of their skills.

Goals

1. Learning to Live.
2. Learning to Learn.
3. Learning to Make a Living.

Career Education is *NOT*

1. Another name for vocational education.
2. "Anti-college" or "Pro Trade Skills."
3. Another course to be stuffed into the existing curriculum.
4. Concerned with "locking-in" a student at an early age to any particular career or occupational group.
5. General education.
6. Strictly a school responsibility.
7. The responsibility of a "guidance program."
8. Limited to non-college bound students.

LOWER SCHOOL

Objectives

1. Develop in pupils positive attitudes about the personal and social significance of work.
2. Develop each pupil's self-awareness in relation to his environment.
3. Develop and expand the occupational awareness and the aspirations of the pupils.
4. Improve overall pupil performance by unifying and focusing basic subjects around a career development theme.
5. Develop each student's ability to make decisions wisely.

MIDDLE SCHOOL

Objectives

1. Provide experiences for students to assist them to evaluate their interests, abilities, values and needs as they relate to aspirations leading to occupational roles.
2. Provide students with opportunities for further and more detailed exploration of selected occupational clusters, leading to the tentative selection of a particular cluster for in-depth exploration at the upper school level.
3. Improve the performance of students in basic subject areas by making the subject matter more meaningful and relevant through unifying and focusing it around a career development theme.

UPPER SCHOOL

Objectives

1. Provide in-depth exploration and training in an occupational cluster leading to entry-level skills in at least one occupation and providing a foundation for further progress, leaving open the option to change occupations or clusters if desired.
2. Improve the performance of students in basic subject areas by making the subject matter more meaningful and relevant through unifying and focusing it around a career development theme.
3. Provide guidance and counseling for the purpose of assisting students in selecting an occupational specialty to prepare them for employment and/or further education.
4. Increase the students' motivation to learn by relating their studies to their future.
5. Placement opportunities for all students, upon leaving school, in either:
   a. A job.
   b. A post-secondary occupational education program.
   c. A four-year college program.
6. Maintain continuous follow-through of students, both dropouts and graduates, to assess effectiveness of programs and to use the resulting information for program improvement. (17: not numbered)

Field programs sponsored by the Pennsylvania Department of Education reflect the view of career education presented in the above statements.

LOCAL LEVEL

An examination of published statements of local-level career education programs and proposals revealed that a surprising number of districts have failed to include a formal definition of the meaning of career education. Consequently, it is difficult to make an accurate assessment of intended program adjustments and changes. Research of proposed learning activities, however, indicates that most programs are assuming a definite vocational attitude at all levels. In the name of career education, many districts have identified certain areas of emphasis such as occupational awareness, occupational exploration, and occupational specialization and have assigned these areas to the elementary school, junior high or middle school, senior high school, and post-secondary education, respectively.

Some local programs are instituted at the upper elementary grade level. The argument presented is that the primary school is appropriately assigned the task of instructing children in the basic skills, and the accomplishments through such efforts as units on "community helpers" meet the career education needs of youngsters. Some districts seem to be giving new labels to existing programs as the only change needed to claim allegiance to the career education movement.

Several school districts are in the process of defining, designing, and implementing complete career education programs that reflect concern for children and sophisticated educational thought.

The same reporting difficulties encountered in state programs were found in local-level programs.

Beaverton, Oregon.   Career educators in the Beaverton Public Schools have developed a formal definition that requires little commentary:

> Career education is a developmental process which is designed to help all individuals prepare for their life roles: vocational, economic, community, home and avocational. Career education enables students to examine their abilities, interests and aptitudes; relate them to career opportunities; and make valid decisions regarding further education and/or work.
>
> Career education becomes a part of all levels of education from kindergarten through adult life. The elementary school years will provide awareness of the world of work and an understanding of the value of work to the individual and family. Through the junior high years, the student will explore and try out his talents and interests and make tentative occupational and educational choices. The high school years will provide an opportunity for the student to prepare for entry into a broad occupational area and/or advanced educational programs after high school. Postsecondary programs will provide for specialized training, upgrading of skills, and retraining opportunities.
>
> Career education is not a separate course in the school curriculum, nor is it an isolated activity. It is a current, ongoing, activity-oriented process incorporated throughout the curriculum, and designed to help the individual develop the skills and knowledge for effective participation in all life roles. (1: not numbered)

Dallas, Texas.   The Skyline Center for Career Development in Dallas has resulted from the efforts of the Dallas Independent School District and the Dallas community and from a general dedication to making education more meaningful and more relevant for the community's high school students. The Center also provides educational services in greater variety to all citizens of the Dallas area. It is housed in a $21 million facility designed to compliment instruction in a cluster-based system.

Even though the following quotation is not a formal definition of career education, it does give the reader an awareness of how career education is regarded in the Dallas program:

> With full knowledge of the magnitude of the mission, educational leaders of the DISD have set out to *expand educational opportunities in Dallas,* and *to help provide each citizen with the preparation necessary to enter the career field of his choice.* Toward these ends Skyline Center personnel recognize learning as ongoing, evolving processes shared by administrators, teachers, students, and the Dallas Community. To accomplish this

Skyline is pledged to foster an atmosphere conducive to creative growth and development in concepts, skills and interpersonal relationships. . . . At the core of Skyline's Career Development Center (CDC) is the goal of *extensive preparation in career education*. . . . *Individualization of Instruction* is basic to Skyline's instructional program with major emphasis on development of skills and content. . . .Skyline's communication program and Center for Community Services help fulfill the goal of *Involvement of Community*. . . . A basic intent is for Skyline to be recognized as a *catalyst for positive educational change*. (3:1–2)

Fort Benton, Montana.   In this small rural school district, a K–12 program called "Preparation and Counseling for the World of Work" has been funded under ESEA Title III and has been organized around career education mini-courses. The program intends to ". . . (1) assist elementary children in developing an understanding about themselves, their values, and an appreciation for all types of work in the world in which they live; (2) develop the affective, psychomotive, as well as the cognitive growth of the individual through the mini-courses; (3) provide the student with a satisfaction of needs which will be necessary eventually for a realistic occupational choice."

The basic goals of "Preparation and Counseling for the World of Work" are:

1. Develop an appreciation for the world of work.
2. Develop an understanding of the individual through self-awareness.
3. Develop an emotional and aesthetic maturity through the exposure to the world of work mini-courses.
4. Develop self-confidence, sense of belonging, personality and character.
5. Develop a positive attitude through guidance towards all aspects of the world of work.
6. Develop a knowledge of how different jobs affect individual and living patterns of families.
7. Develop an understanding for the relationship of interests and abilities involved in different occupations.
8. Develop an appreciation for natural environment and its effect upon the world of work.
9. Develop a knowledge of the interdependency of consumer attitudes upon the world of work.
10. Develop an aptitude for making wise use of leisure time. (6.vi)

Hackensack, New Jersey.   The Hackensack career education program could be called a national project because of its relationship to the Comprehensive Career Education Model (CCEM) developmental project except that it was selected for the quality of the career education project developed prior to being considered by CCEM. As a member of the CCEM project, career education in Hackensack is guided in part by the tenets listed on page 8. The program calls for career education to ". . . begin as soon as the student entered school. From the earliest grades onward they would be led to see the relevance of their classroom studies to the world of work. . . ." Included in the definition of the Hackensack program must be the following statements from the Comprehensive Education Matrix:

1. It is essential that each person know himself and develop a personal value system.
2. It is essential that each person perceive the relationship between education and life roles.
3. It is essential that each person acquire knowledge of the wide range of careers.
4. It is essential that each person be able to perceive processes in production, distribution, and consumption relative to his economic environment.
5. It is essential that each person be able to use information in determining alternatives and reaching decisions.
6. It is essential that each person acquire and develop skills which are viewed as ways in which man extends his behavior.
7. It is essential that each person develop social and communication skills appropriate to career placement and adjustment.
8. It is essential that each person develop appropriate feelings toward self and others.

In turn, the key concepts provide the basis for the eight elements of career education which comprise a significant part of the Matrix. These are:

1. Self-Awareness
2. Educational Awareness
3. Career Awareness
4. Economic Awareness
5. Decision Making
6. Beginning Competency
7. Employable Skills
8. Attitudes and Appreciations (9: not numbered)

Riverton, Wyoming.   Riverton's career education program was implemented by expanding the existing program rather than adding totally new curriculum components. The curricular expansion was designed to: (1) promote understanding of occupations, (2) provide occupational information, (3) explore the world of work, and (4) help students learn about themselves. The Riverton definition is centered around four major characteristics:

1. *Career education is designed to acquaint individuals with career opportunities and options.*

   Presenting career information to students is the responsibility of the entire school staff. Unbiased and realistic career information should be integrated into all subject matter content offered individuals at all levels.

2. *Career education is designed to assist individuals in developing a realistic self-concept.*

   Activities and/or experiences must be provided which will aid individuals in developing a realistic self-concept. How an individual perceives himself, how others perceive him, and what he perceives as an ideal self, often relates directly to expressed career interests. The comprehensiveness and accuracy of data possessed by the individual should lead to more rational decision making.

3. *Career education is designed to aid individuals in making career preferences and or choices.*

   Individuals should be extended the opportunity to explore career preferences to the depth desired. Coordination of school and community resources is necessary if individuals are to develop positive attitudes toward the world of work and realistic images of persons in the work world.

4. *Career education provides the vehicle for the development of such skills and abilities as are needed so that the individual might achieve his career goals.*

   Learning experiences should be structured to give the individual those skills and abilities as are needed so that he might achieve his career preference with the flexibility to change career direction without academic penalty. Career education emphasizes an employable product. (19:1)

DEFINITIONS BY INDIVIDUALS

Individual educators who have enthusiasm for the career education movement have provided another source of definitions. Some of these are not complete formal definitions and some must be gleaned a phrase at a time from the writings of the individual, but many of them are complete and concise statements of meaning. Goldhammer offered one such definition that is centered around human capacitation:

> The purposes of education must be stated in terms of the individual learner and what he does as a result of engagement in the educational enterprise. From this point of view, the *primary purpose of education is to assist the student to become a fully capacitated, self-motivating, self-fulfilled, contributing member of society. . . . Fully capacitated* means that the school shall assist the student to perform all of his life roles with the skill, knowledge, and understanding necessary in all of them. (7:125–26)

Goldhammer identified the following life roles or life careers around which capacitation is developed and gave centrality of importance to the first one:

1. A producer of goods or a renderer of services.
2. A member of a family group.
3. A participant in social and political life of society.
4. A participant in avocational pursuits.
5. A participant in the regulatory functions involved in aesthetic, moral and religious concerns. (7:129)

Closely related to the life roles are the objectives of Goldhammer's careers curriculum:

1. Social effectiveness
2. Economic productivity
3. Self-realization
4. Moral responsibility (7:128–129)

Goldhammer, in collaboration with Taylor, incorporated the above characteristics into a formal definition:

> Specifically, career education is designed to capacitate individuals for their several life roles: economic, community, home, avocational, religious, and aesthetic. It recognizes the centrality of careers in shaping our lives by determining or limiting where we work, where we live, our associates and other dimensions that are significant in defining our life style. Designed for all students, career education should be viewed as lifelong and pervasive, permeating the entire school program and even extending beyond it. (8:6)

According to Hoyt, Evans, Mackin, and Mangum, career education is a total concept, a way of preparing for and maintaining a "lifelong, productive career," without diminishing other aspects of learning and living:

> A career is a personally satisfying succession of productive activities hinged together over a lifetime and generally leading toward greater satisfaction and contribution. Therefore, career education is preparation for all meaningful and productive activity, at work or at leisure, whether paid or volunteer, as employee or employer, in private business or in the public sector, or in the family. The key words are "productivity" and "achievement." (10:2)

> Career education is not something that precedes participating in society but is an integration of learning and doing that merges the worlds of the home, the community, the school, and the workplace into a challenging and productive whole. . . . It offers a salable skill at any port of entry into the job market, yet keeps the doors open to return for further upgrading

and progression or change of career direction. Rather than a lock step, kindergarten-through-12th or-14th or-16th year ladder, it is better thought of as a broad freeway with convenient exits and reentries as interests and needs change. (10:3)

Career education's goal is to make work possible, meaningful, and satisfactory to every individual, for the best measure of man is what he achieves and how he serves. (10:4)

Hoyt, et al. go on to identify eight key concepts that further define career education and the philosophy upon which it is based:

1. Preparation for successful working careers shall be a key objective of all education.
2. Every teacher in every course will emphasize the contribution that subject matter can make to a successful career.
3. "Hands-on" occupationally oriented experiences will be utilized as a method of teaching and motivating the learning of abstract academic content.
4. Preparation for careers will be recognized as the mutual importance of work attitudes, human relations skills, orientation to the nature of the workaday world, exposure to alternative career choices, and the acquisition of actual job skills.
5. Learning will not be reserved for the classroom, but learning environments for career education will also be identified in the home, the community, and employing establishments.
6. Beginning in early childhood and continuing through the regular school years, allowing the flexibility for a youth to leave for experience and return to school for further education (including opportunity for upgrading and continued refurbishing for adult workers and including productive use of leisure time and the retirement years), career education will seek to extend its time horizons from "womb to tomb."
7. Career education is a basic and pervasive approach to all education, but it in no way conflicts with other legitimate education objectives such as citizenship, culture, family responsibility, and basic education.
8. The schools cannot shed responsibility for the individual just because he has been handed a diploma or has dropped out. While it may not perform the actual placement function, the school has the responsibility to stick with the youth until he has his feet firmly on the next step of his career ladder, help him get back on the ladder if his foot slips, and be available to help him onto a new ladder at any point in the future that one proves to be too short or unsteady. (10:5-6)

Reinhart, in summarizing his paper, "Nature and Characteristics of Emerging Career Education Curriculum" defined a career education curriculum that would contribute to finding a practical solution to educational and vocational problems:

The emerging careers curriculum is organized around a functional priority of life roles (careers). The vocational career provides the central focus of the careers curriculum; although other careers involving the family, social and political life, avocational pursuits, and the regulatory functions of aesthetic, moral, and religious concerns are also considered necessary to an adequate careers curriculum. Whatever else it is, the emergence of the careers curriculum is a socially and politically conservative phenomenon which affirms the role of social maintenance of the public schools.

The emerging careers curriculum purports to integrate the entire school curriculum—academic, general, and vocational—in such a way that all education will be functionally related to the performance of career roles. In its attempt to create a functional unity, it must confront the long-standing strife between educators over the education of the "specialist type of man" and the older, "cultivated man." The strategy, however, is not to force confrontations between traditionally incompatible disciplines, but to combine the pedagogical heritage of the past and the technical sophistication of the present to create a unified educational system that has a relevant academic curriculum and a humanistic vocational one. (18:14)

Elementary school principals attending a summer workshop in careers education at Oregon State University included statements of definition as a part of individually prepared outlines of proposed career education programs:

Careers education is the sum total process of family, community, and public school learning experiences by which each individual child early in his life becomes aware of the values of the working society about him, by which he explores his own choice of a vocation, and by which he eventually makes his lifework a satisfying, useful, and meaningful part of his personal life.

Career education becomes the concept of providing a more meaningful education so that each student will be helped to develop a sound decision-making procedure based on his values, will be able to evaluate alternatives of directions and understand his rights and responsibilities as a member of society and to fulfill his careers (roles of family, citizen, vocation and avocation) in a meaningful manner.

At the elementary level of career education, the vocation role focuses on the awareness level of vocations. This awareness can be integrated into the present curriculum by changing the emphasis of how workers are discussed and presented. The emphasis becomes on the role of the worker as a whole person not on the product of the worker.

Career education is a developmental process designed to help all individuals prepare for their life roles in the world of work: family; citizenship; vocation; avocation. This process provides each student an opportunity to examine his or her abilities and aptitudes, interests, and attitudes and relate them to careers enabling each to make valid decisions regarding their future education and productive life roles.

> Career education is an all inclusive educational delivery system that permits a child to develop according to his abilities and interests, his citizenship responsibilities, occupational readiness, and moral and physical development. The child is exposed to educational experiences that will help him enjoy full, functional living in the present and in the future. (4:1-4)

The incorporation of career education into on-going educational programs is being accomplished in a variety of ways. The historic way of bringing new programs into the elementary school has been to add it on as a new appendage to an already overcrowded body. It is suspected that history is repeating itself in the case of career education and that some elementary teachers are being told by administrators to crowd one more activity into instructional programs that ceased to be effective long ago, because of the lack of careful planning that is characteristic of strong educational leadership. It is easy to believe that in schools where this means of incorporation is being employed, career education will fail to achieve its intended purposes and may in fact detract from the achievement of other educational objectives.

At the secondary level, the process of curricular change, for more than a few schools, has been to add or delete courses in terms of available staff and the interest of individual instructors. Undoubtedly, in a number of junior and senior high schools, new courses are being added whose titles reflect a content that in some way is concerned with careers. Faculties who wish to express concern for career education make these new courses required. In other schools, students have one more elective to ponder. In either case, the intent of career education has been ignored to the detriment of possible gains in relevant learning.

Obviously, there are better ways of making career education a part of existing programs than those discussed in this chapter. In many schools where career education has been adopted by the faculty as an important educational thrust, the entire program has been revamped in order to make the new direction a total learning experience. Administrators who have been successful in converting conventional school programs to career education have devised ways of involving all those concerned with the education process—parents, members of the community, members of the business-professional-industrial world, students, teachers, and administrators—in rewriting philosophies, redefining objectives, planning new activities, and preparing and selecting additional materials. They have assisted in developing appropriate evaluation procedures to meet the demands of assessing student growth and achievement, assuring continuous program improvement, and providing the data of accountability; and they have patiently helped teachers overcome the frustration and trauma of finding human purpose in the teaching of subject matter. They have been true educational leaders and only through such leadership can career education, or any educational program, make significant contributions to the fulfillment of learners and improvement of our way of life.

REFERENCES

1. Beaverton Public Schools. "Career Education." (Statement of definition prepared by the district) Beaverton, Oregon, 1972.

2. Chasnoff, Robert E. *Elementary Curriculum: A Book of Readings.* New York: Pitman, 1964.

3. Dallas Independent School District. "Skyline Center." Dallas: The Center, 1972. (Mimeo-2 pages)

4. Division of Elementary Education. "Career Education: Workshop for Elementary Principals." Corvallis: Oregon State University, August 1972.

5. Elliot, Ian. "Occupational Orientation Means Work for You." *Grade Teacher,* April 1971.

6. Fort Benton Public Schools. *Preparation and Counseling for the World of Work.* Fort Benton, Montana: The School District, 1972.

7. Goldhammer, Keith. "A Careers Curriculum." In Keith Goldhammer and Robert E. Taylor, *Career Education: Perspective and Promise.* Columbus, Ohio: Charles E. Merrill, 1972.

8. Goldhammer, Keith and Robert E. Taylor. *Career Education: Perspective and Promise.* Columbus, Ohio: Charles E. Merrill, 1972.

9. Hackensack School District. "The Hackensack Career Education Center." Hackensack: The Center, 1972. (Mimeo)

10. Hoyt, Kenneth B., Rupert W. Evans, Edward F. Mackin, and Garth L. Mangum. *Career Education: What It Is and How To Do It.* Salt Lake City: Olympus, 1972.

11. Idaho State Department of Education and Idaho State Department of Vocational Education. "Guidelines for a Comprehensive Educational Program for the State of Idaho." Boise: State Department of Education, 1972. (Mimeo)

12. Kunzman, Leonard E. "Career Education in Oregon." Salem, Oregon: Oregon Board of Education, 1970.

13. _____. *State Plan for Vocational Education.* Salem, Oregon: Oregon Board of Education, 1972.

14. Marland, Sidney P., "Career Education: Equipping Students for the World of Work," *College and University Business,* December 1971.

15. Miller, A. J. *School Based Comprehensive Career Education Model.* Columbus: The Center for Vocational and Technical Education, The Ohio State University, 1972.

16. National Association of State Directors of Vocational Education. *A Position Paper on Career Education.* Washington, D.C.: The Association, 1971.

17. Pennsylvania Department of Education. "Career Education." Harrisburg: The Department, 1972. (Mimeo)

18. Reinhart, Bruce. "Nature and Characteristics of Emerging Career Education." Columbus: The Center for Vocational and Technical Education, The Ohio State University, 1972.

19. School District No. 28, Riverton, Wyoming. "Career Education Program K-14." Riverton, Wyoming: The Project, 1972.

20. South Carolina Region V Educational Service Center. *South Carolina Exemplary Project in Career Education.* Lancaster: The Center, 1972.

21. U. S. Department of Health, Education and Welfare, "Career Education." DHEW Publication No. (OE) 12-39. Washington, D.C.: U. S. Government Printing Office, 1971.

22. Wolfe, Don M. *The Image of Man in America.* New York: Crowell, 1970.

Chapter 2 ELEMENTARY SCHOOL CAREERS EDUCATION MODEL

Introduction

The public school career education model that has received the most attention nationally was constructed as a ladder that has as its first rung *career awareness* in the elementary school. The junior high or middle school step deals with *career exploration* and at the high school level students participate in programs of *occupational preparation.* Progress up the ladder at the post-high school and adult levels is focused on *occupational specialization.* (See figure 2–1).

An example of a ladder program is the Career Education Model developed by the Department of Career Education of the Oregon Board of Education. It has been entitled "The Oregon Way" and is constructed as a pyramid that has Elementary Career Awareness as its base and climaxes with Occupational Specialization. The Oregon model is organized around the following developmental levels:

Career Awareness (Grades K–6)

Includes programs in the elementary grades, where students will:

—develop awareness of the many occupational careers available

—develop awareness of self in relation to the occupation career role

—develop foundations for wholesome attitudes toward work and society

—develop attitudes of respect and appreciation toward workers in all fields

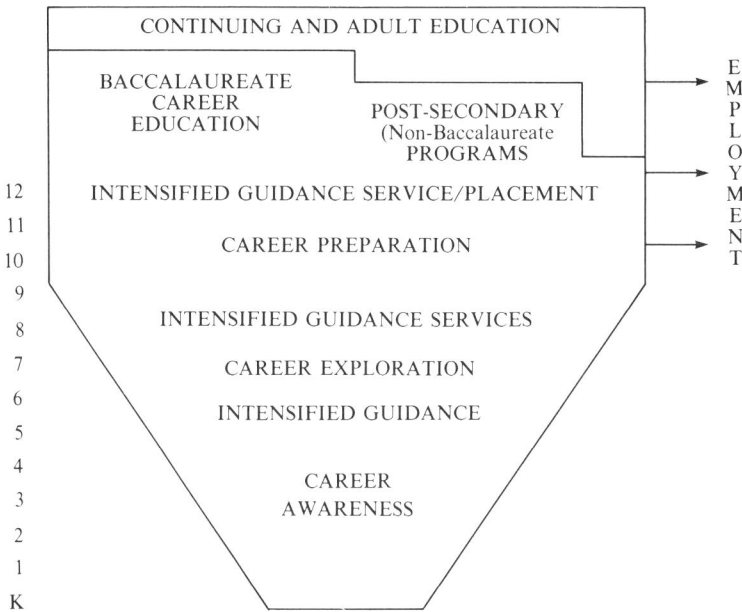

```
┌─────────────────────────────────────────────────┐
│         CONTINUING AND ADULT EDUCATION          │
│  ┌────────────────────┐                         │
│  BACCALAUREATE         │                         │      E
│    CAREER              │                         │      M
│   EDUCATION      POST-SECONDARY                  │      P
│                (Non-Baccalaureate               │→     L
│                  PROGRAMS                        │      O
│                                                  │      Y
    INTENSIFIED GUIDANCE SERVICE/PLACEMENT         │→     M
                                                          E
              CAREER PREPARATION                   │→     N
                                                          T

          INTENSIFIED GUIDANCE SERVICES

             CAREER EXPLORATION

             INTENSIFIED GUIDANCE

                    CAREER
                  AWARENESS
```

12
11
10
9
8
7
6
5
4
3
2
1
K

FIGURE 2–1

A COMPREHENSIVE CAREER EDUCATION SYSTEM (1:18)

—make tentative choices of career cluster to explore in greater depth during mid-school years

Career Exploration (Grades 7–10)

Programs in the mid-school years usually grades 6–7 through 10, where students will:

—explore key occupational areas and assess own interests and abilities

—become familiar with occupational classifications and clusters

—develop awareness of relevant factors to be considered in decision-making

—gain experience in meaningful decision-making

—develop tentative occupational plans and arrive at a tentative career choice

Occupational Preparation (Grades 11–12)

Centers on Career Cluster programs at grades 11–12 where students will:

—acquire occupational skills and knowledge for entry level employment and/or advanced occupational training

—tie a majority of high school experiences into generalized career goals

—develop acceptable job attitudes

—be involved in cooperative work experience and have opportunity to be a member of a vocational youth organization

Occupational Specialization (Post-High School and Adult)

Includes programs in:

13 community colleges

Apprenticeship

Private Vo-Tech Schools

4-year colleges and universities

Where students will:

—be involved in developing specific occupational knowledge and preparation in a specialized job area

—have opportunity to form meaningful employer-employee type relationships

—be provided necessary retraining or upgrading skills (2:1)

Guidance and counseling services in the Oregon model are available to all students at all levels.

The "Career Cluster" concept is usually incorporated into the model at one or more levels and may be described as an organizational arrangement designed to enhance communications in career education. It is a means of grouping occupational titles into clusters representing related occupations. All levels of occupations are included from entry-level jobs that require the least preparation to those skilled and technical jobs that require maximum preparation and experience. The clusters also represent jobs that have had a continuing importance and, based on current information, will continue to benefit our society. The U. S. Office of Education has identified the following fifteen groups of occupations in a cluster scheme that makes it possible to give consideration to every job listed in the *Dictionary of Occupational Titles:*

Construction Occupations Cluster

Manufacturing Occupations Cluster

Transportation Occupations Cluster

Agri-Business and Natural Resources Occupations Cluster

Marine Science Occupations Cluster

Environmental Occupations Cluster

Business and Office Occupations Cluster

Marketing and Distribution Occupations Cluster

Communications and Media Occupations Cluster

Hospitality and Recreation Occupations Cluster

Personal Service Occupations Cluster

Public Service Occupations Cluster

Health Occupations Cluster
Consumer and Homemaking Occupations Cluster
Fine Arts and Humanistic Occupations Cluster

The emphasis in most models is on preparation for occupations. Even though model designers state that career education must be both pervasive and comprehensive, little actual attention is given to preparation for careers other than those generally classified as skilled and technical occupations.

A goal of career education that reflects one of the primary reasons given for including career development in the schools is to increase job possibilities for the majority of students whose post-school needs have not been considered in traditional education programs. Ignored in attempting to achieve this goal is preparation for the professions and for the life roles that contribute to vocational career success and to personal fulfillment. These areas of preparation are mentioned in some narrative introductions to career education models, but they are generally omitted in the detailed working descriptions of the programs.

Elementary school career education is included in a majority of models but it receives far less attention than its importance warrants. The success of the total careers education program depends upon the introduction and development of basic skills, attitudes, and knowledge at the elementary level. Any program that excludes the elementary school or restricts its role to the consideration of transient occupational trivia misses the intent of careers education and reflects a gross ignorance of both human and career development.

The Elementary School Careers Education Model

The position taken in developing the elementary school careers education model is that if life is to be a truly fulfilling experience, individuals must experience a degree of success in all aspects of living, and that public education should make a significant contribution to growth and development in major life roles. Consequently, the model has as its organizing theme the life careers that have the greatest influence on living in America. These major life careers have been identified as: career as a family member, career as a citizen, career as a member of a vocation, and career as a pursuer of avocational interests. Thus the model is a careers model rather than a career model.

The model has been challenged on the basis that there is a difference between "career" and "life role" and that only the vocational component is worthy of being designated a career. Such a position is acceptable for programs and schools designed exclusively to prepare students to enter an occupation, but elementary education is based on a much broader set of purposes. The curriculum of the elementary school should be "life" and the method of learning should be "living." The purpose of elementary education should be to help children gain in their ability to live fully all components of their lives.

Certain assumptions are basic to the use of the life careers as the focal point of the model. First, living does not break down neatly into discrete elements. Living is a total experience in which performance in one component can influence success in other components. The model must therefore consider the interrelationships that should be developed among the careers. Second, education programs should give approximately the same attention to the development of each career, because of the impact each career has on the life style of individuals and because of the possible detrimental effect inadequate preparation in one career could have on total life success. Thus, the model assumes an attitude of equality among the careers. Third, people need to be successful in as many of the factors of living as possible and for those who, by choice or because of the circumstances of their lives, are not members of an occupation, there should be dignity in seeking success in other life careers. Fourth, the four careers are evident in the lives of children and give meaning and relevant organization to elementary education. Fifth, ignoring or relegating a component of living to a subordinate or inferior position in the school program does more to destroy its chances of development than it contributes to the development of the component given supremacy. This condition permits a feeling of success among school people who have only participated in the development of one aspect of happy productive living. If elementary education is to make a significant difference in the lives of children, programs must be capable of advancing the "whole child" and total living.

The three-dimensional model offered here is an attempt to develop educational relationships among factors of living, elements of learning, and components of curriculum. It is an effort to give organization and unification to elementary education in a way that is understandable and credible to educators, lay people, and children. The diagrammatic model presented in Figures 2–2 through 2–5 is an attempt to give visual interpretation to the elementary careers education program. The graphic model is intended for use at the local level in several ways:

1. The total model can be used as a means of initiating the in-service discussions that must precede any decision to accept careers education into the local schools.

2. The total model can also be employed as a basis for organizing the staff into in-service groups for purposes of investigating the various elements of career education.

3. The lists of elements that appear as axes in the single-dimension matrices (Figures 2–2, 2–3, and 2–4) can provide a point of begin-

ning in the identification of those elements of living, learning, and curriculum that are most appropriate for inclusion in the local model.

4. The "cells" of the model offer a view of how instruction and materials can be organized.

5. The cells can be used as a guide for inventorying both the quantity and the appropriateness of existing materials for careers education. The inventory may influence the nature of the adopted model.

6. The cells can also be the means of relating the many details of the existing program to careers education and of evaluating the relationship between the present and the new program.

The four life careers are discussed in detail in chapter 30. Chapter 4 is an elaboration of the five elements of learning and the permeating influences.

Figure 2–2 represents the first dimension of the elementary careers education model. The vertical axis is made up of the identified elements of learning; self-concept, human relationships, intellectual power, continuous learning, and knowledge acquisition. The horizontal axis is formed listing the factors of living: family, citizen, vocation, and avocation. The content of the cells (1A through 5D) is composed of goals, concepts, skills, knowledge, methods, materials, ideas, ideals, and a host of activities and experiences needed to develop and make permanent the living and learning relationship indicated by the vertical and horizontal cell titles.

The content of cell 1A, for example, is concerned with the family career and with self-concept. The learning task is to design experiences that will promote an individual's self-concept as a family member. Accomplishment of the task, and development of the cell requires identification of the knowledge needed to understand family and family roles, the skills needed to seek and to maintain a rewarding position in the family for self and others, and the attitudes basic to trust and human acceptance. Cells 1B, 1C, and 1D challenge the program designer to provide for improving self-concept in each of the other three careers.

An examination of the learning requirements of cell 2A provides an opportunity to break down the compartmentalized appearance of the cells and view the overlapping, integrated relationship that exists among the cells. Cell 2A deals with human relations in the family. In identifying learning experiences appropriate to the achievement of the goal of the cell, the line between cells 1A and 2A must disintegrate; for self-indentity in the family is a matter of human relationships. No cell in the model is or can be strictly self-contained.

In the second dimension of the elementary careers model (figure 2–3), eight curricular areas are listed in the horizontal axis while the five elements of learning remain in the same vertical position they held in Figure 2–2. The relationship developed in the cells in this dimension is concerned with employing the various subject areas as the vehicle by which the elements

LIVING ╲ LEARNING	A FAMILY	B CITIZEN	C VOCATION	D AVOCATION	
1 SELF-CONCEPT	1-A	1-B	1-C	1-D	←
2 HUMAN RELATIONSHIP	2-A	2-B	2-C	2-D	←
3 INTELLECTUAL POWER	3-A	3-B	3-C	3-D	
4 CONTINUOUS LEARNING	4-A	4-B	4-C	4-D	←
5 KNOWLEDGE ACQUISITION	5-A	5-B	5-C	5-D	

P E R M E A T I N G   I N F L U E N C E S

↑ ↑ ↑

PERMEATING INFLUENCES
AESTHETICS
MORAL
SPIRITUAL
PHYSICAL

FIGURE 2–2

ELEMENTARY CAREERS EDUCATION MODEL: FIRST DIMENSION

of learning are presented to children. The content of the cells should reflect a concern for establishing a relationship between the elements of learning and curricular areas that give practicality and permanence to the goals of learning and leaves the greatest subject matter residue. The educational questions in need of answers in cells 1-II through 1-VIII are: what are the instructional approaches, materials, and learning experiences capable of making the most effective use of the various subject areas; and how can the development of self-concept also result in mastery of subject matter and give permanence to an element of learning that is often transient?

CURRICULUM / LEARNING	I ART	II HEALTH P. E.	III LANGUAGE ARTS	IV MATHE-MATICS	V MUSIC	VI READING	VII SCIENCE	VIII SOCIAL STUDIES
1 SELF-CONCEPT	1-I	1-II	1-III	1-IV	1-V	1-VI	1-VII	1-VIII
2 HUMAN RELATIONSHIPS	2-I	2-II	2-III	2-IV	2-V	2-VI	2-VII	2-VIII
3 INTELLECTUAL POWER	3-I	3-II	3-III	3-IV	3-V	3-VI	3-VII	3-VIII
4 CONTINUOUS LEARNING	4-I	4-II	4-III	4-IV	4-V	4-VI	4-VII	4-VIII
5 KNOWLEDGE ACQUISITION	5-I	5-II	5-III	5-IV	5-V	5-VI	5-VII	5-VIII

PERMEATING INFLUENCES →

PERMEATING INFLUENCES

AESTHETICS
MORAL
SPIRITUAL
PHYSICAL

FIGURE 2–3

ELEMENTARY CAREERS EDUCATION MODEL: SECOND DIMENSION

The explanation of the mechanics of the third dimension of the model (figure 2–4) is similar to that given for the other dimensions. The life careers appear in the horizontal axis and the curricular areas form the vertical axis. Curricular areas are evaluated in terms of the possible use that can be made of related subject matter in helping children achieve success in each of the careers. Success in the careers, if the contents of the cells have been accurately determined, should also mean success in acquiring the knowledge available in the subject areas.

Figure 2–5 incorporates the dimensions discussed above into a three-dimensional model that represents the total careers education program. All components of the program (careers, learning, and curriculum) are integrated in the cells. Thus, cell 1-A-II brings together family, self-concept, and art; and cell 5-D-VIII unites avocation, knowledge acquisition, and social studies. The model might give a more accurate picture if it could appear as a sphere rather than as a cube for it is a cyclic arrangement in which each component is instructionally combined at some point with all other components.

LIVING \ LEARNING	A FAMILY	B CITIZEN	C VOCATION	D AVOCATION	
I ART	I-A	I-B	I-C	I-D	
II HEALTH P. E.	II-A	II-B	II-C	II-D	← P E R M E A T I N G
III LANGUAGE ARTS	III-A	III-B	III-C	III-D	
IV MATHEMATICS	IV-A	IV-B	IV-C	IV-D	← I N F L U E N C E S
V MUSIC	V-A	V-B	V-C	V D	
VI READING	VI-A	VI-B	VI-C	VI-D	
VII SCIENCE	VII-A	VII-B	VII-C	VII-D	←
VIII SOCIAL STUDIES	VIII-A	VIII-B	VIII-C	VIII-D	

↑　　　↑　　　　　　↑

PERMEATING INFLUENCES

AESTHETICS
MORAL
SPIRITUAL
PHYSICAL

FIGURE 2–4

ELEMENTARY CAREERS EDUCATION MODEL: THIRD DIMENSION

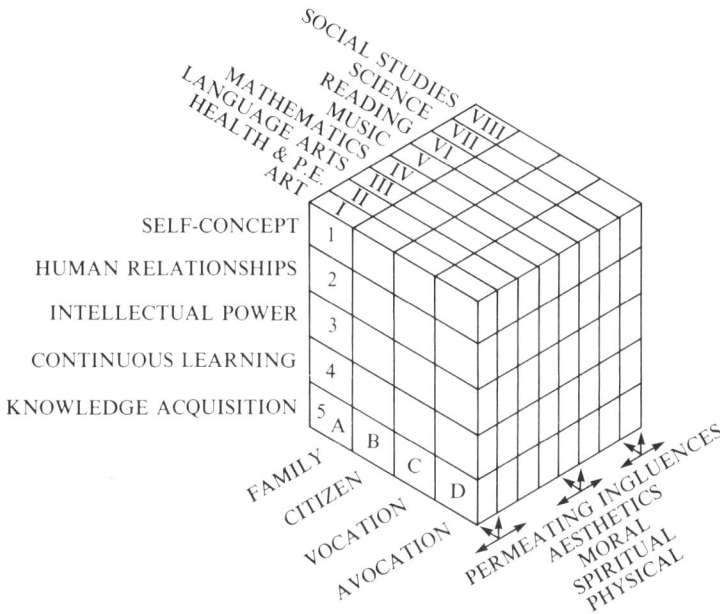

FIGURE 2-5

ELEMENTARY CAREERS EDUCATION: A COMPREHENSIVE MODEL

The elementary careers model has been organized as a spiral rather than as a ladder. The model provides for the knowledge, skills, and attitudes introduced to children in the early school years to be re-encountered at all levels in increasingly more complex and demanding learning experiences. Awareness, exploration, and preparation, for example, are continuously developed at all levels, rather than being assigned to specific levels. Because children are provided opportunities to apply earlier learning to meeting needs that are constantly changing, they become more sophisticated in all aspects of their physical, social, and intellectual performance. For this reason, the three-dimensional model is appropriate for all levels and development of the content of the cells should make provision for the presentation of all components at all levels.

Permeating the entire model are those influences that give meaning and consistency to life. Spiritual and moral values and aesthetics are of primary concern in developing each cell of the model. The intensity of the concern is maintained consistently from component to component and from cell to cell. The success of the model is dependent upon individuals finding opportunities to develop principles by which to direct the affairs of their lives. The degree of success is influenced by the learner's desire to see beauty and his ability to find it in all aspects and associations of living, particularly in other human beings. This concern appears in the graphic model as "Permeating Influences."

In summary, the development of the contents of each cell in each dimension of the model, when integrated with the content of cells in other dimensions, produces the content of the cells in the three-dimensional model. This is not a hard and fast educational "system" that is complete and capable of maximum performance when all the cells are filled. It is intended to be only a systematic and understandable way of viewing an educational program and a guide to making decisions about teaching children. It is not an organization into which children are "plugged" and out of which they emerge in possession of predetermined knowledge and behavior. It is a means of ensuring that all phases of childhood development are accounted for in a flexible and creative way that respects individuality and human dignity. The model was constructed to benefit the adults who are responsible for educating our young. It was not intended to impose an unnatural order on the way children learn or an unreal organization to the manner in which children live.

No school should attempt to do more than it is capable of doing well in terms of its staff, facilities, and financial resources. Neither should educators adopt a model just because it is available, or borrow an educational program on the basis of its reported success in another location. The model adopted and made operational at the local level should be a professional interpretation of the needs of children and the community in which they live and of the educational capabilities of the district. This is not to deny the value of examining programs and models developed by others as a means of enhancing local educational efforts; it is a reminder that children require programs that are unique to their needs, interests, and capabilities.

The elementary careers education model does not pretend to represent all possible alternatives in elementary education or give undue importance to those that are represented. It represents an educational program in need of local interpretation and adjustment.

REFERENCES

1. Miller, A. J. The Emerging School Based Comprehensive Education Model." Columbus: The Center for Vocational and Technical Education, The Ohio State University, 1972.

2. Oregon Board of Education. "The Oregon Way." Salem, Oregon: Oregon Board of Education, 1972. (Brochure)

Chapter 3 THE CAREERS OF CHILDREN PART I: LIVING

Living and learning cannot be separated. The responsibility of the school is to ensure that they go hand-in-hand in the education of children. Careers education is designed to make learning an experience in living. Educators must identify the factors of living and learning that hold the most importance to the greatest number of people at all ages. The task of the school is to build around these factors a program that offers children unlimited opportunities to realize their maximum potential in each identified area.

The factors identified in chapter 2 are not sacred or necessarily complete. They are offered as a reasonable point of beginning and are worthy of thoughtful consideration in the development of a model of elementary careers education. Deletions, additions, and refinements may be required to make them fit local philosophies and needs. It may be desirable also to reorder them in terms of how local teachers, administrators, and community members react to the contribution they feel each factor should make to achieving school district objectives.

The order in which the careers and factors of learning are presented is based on their importance in the education of elementary school children. Some may be anxious to debate the appropriateness of the order on the grounds that vocation influences life style more than family and therefore should be first rather than third, or it may be argued that the acquisition of knowledge is a more prestigious accomplishment than its last place position indicates. It is understood that no hierarchy of importance could be totally accurate or universally acceptable, which means that this ranking is somewhat arbitrary and in this regard several points need to be made.

First, it is difficult in the lives of children as it is in the lives of adults either to identify or to deny the existence of interrelationships among the careers. It is assumed that success in one career somehow influences success in the other careers and, if this is true, it becomes impossible to assign a ranking to them that would be accurate at all times. Second, that which may be most important in the lives of adults may not be most important in the lives of children. In considering what is important to children from an adult's point of view, the ordering seems appropriate. Third, there is the matter of building upon "where the child is" and what he brings with him to the educational setting. On this basis the ranking in general is acceptable. Finally, there is the question of need. At this point in development, it seems reasonable to believe that knowing self and knowing the significance and importance of family is of greatest need to the elementary school child.

Family Career

The American family has experienced great change in its responsibility for the education of its young during the past 150 years. Changing social and economic conditions have altered the position of the family in our society, as well as the roles of family members and their relationships to one another. The family has moved from a self-sufficient unit that produced most of the goods and services needed by its members, to a unit almost totally dependent upon others for its requirements. The family has ceased to be a producer and has become a consumer. In the process, family members have lost their economic dependence upon one another. Lost too has been the opportunity to develop the skills of human relationship that were so much a part of working together to achieve family goals. The family's loyalty and pride of accomplishment that accompanied the productive efforts of acquiring family needs also has disappeared. Craftsmanship attitudes have undoubtedly suffered as the family lost control of the quality of needed goods and services. And so the shift of the source of goods and services greatly affected the nature of the family and the work attitudes of its members. The shift also created a need for public education to expend substantial effort toward the development of the work-related attitudes that disappeared with the self-sufficient family.

Increased mobility and an ever-increasing availability of social experiences and the addition of new social expectations further dispersed the family. Its members became more dependent upon people and agencies outside the home for their social needs. The result has been greatly altered relationships within the family. In the traditional family, the father was the authority because of superior knowledge and experience. The role of family members was dictated by their position in the line of authority. This authority arrangement has not totally vanished from the American scene but it is no longer appropriate to the family in which the father does many household chores that were once below his position and in which the mother is co-provider or provider. The making of decisions is no longer the sole domain of the male head of the family, but is a shared responsibility in which all members participate. The modern family should have a "companionship arrangement" that serves both the needs of maintaining a household and of providing needed love, human warmth, and security for its members. The need for intimate family relationships did not disappear with the need for families to produce goods and services. As social changes occur within the family and as the need for positive human relationships in all aspects of life becomes more urgent, the school must establish a family atmosphere in which children can develop the skills of living in close proximity to others and reap the rewards of learning to solve the problems of survival with others.

Education of the young in the traditional family had some distinct advantages and was in a very real way careers education. The family was a self-sufficient unit in which children learned the art and science of self-sufficiency from their parent-teachers. Sons almost automatically learned their fathers' ways and means of providing family needs while daughters grew up to keep house in much the same manner as their childhood home was kept. The goals of this family-centered education were known and understood by all, which was a distinct advantage over later formal education. Children understood the importance of the learning they were immediately engaged in because they could relate it to outcomes that were personally significant.

Learning, consequently, was both efficient and effective. It was efficient in that it achieved the desired results in the most economical use of both instructional and learning time and was accomplished with a minimum expenditure of money. It was effective in that it achieved the desired results both in terms of immediate reward to the learner and in terms of his later adult performance. Even though the "good old days" hold little excitement as something to return to, it can be said from a learning point of view that the family system had commendable attributes. Brembeck lists four positive factors of learning found in family-directed education:

> First, the learning in a traditional family took place in a completely natural kind of way. There were no tricks or rewards for motivating the child. Learning took place as a part of the function by which the family lived.

Second, it was easy for the learner . . . to see the relationship between
one small aspect of a task and the whole task. . . . He did not need to be
motivated by extrinsic means. . . . The motivation was instrinsic.

Third, the parents were associated with the young in carrying on work
which was significant to the whole family. . . . Both teaching and learning
flourished in this atmosphere.

Finally, this kind of learning had the *readiness* concept built into it.
(2:131)

One of the results of the evolution of the family has been the removal of
the education of the young from the home to the school, with parents
assuming a decreasing role in the formal education of their offspring. As the
father left the home to find employment in industry and the trades, his
children left home is search of an education that would prepare them to
meet their current and future needs. Unfortunately, an ever-increasing gap
developed between the real needs of children and society and the real (not
stated) outcomes of education. As a result, today there is often little continuity between the values of the home and the community and the values
encouraged by the schools. Learners find themselves in a situation of value
discontinuity causing frustrations that did not exist in the traditional family.
The task of elementary school careers education is to give aid and comfort
to children in their struggle to determine value, and find equilibrium in their
lives by helping them develop lines of continuity between the values of the
home, community, and school.

The current relationship between the child and his family is difficult to
ascertain. Much is written about the fatherless family, the working mother
family, the broken family, the lower class family, the middle class family,
the upper class family, the ethnic minority family, the disadvantaged family,
and a countless number of combinations. Writers have given few compli-
ments to any of these arrangements as appropriate environments in which
to raise children. Some insist that the family influence has eroded to a point
where the welfare of children is threatened. Perkins in discussing the influence of the modern family states that

. . . the family has become a declining influence in the promotion of mental
health and development. Although its members may live under the same
roof, today's family is becoming dispersed—its members drawn out of the
home by little league, scouts, teen-age clubs, cars belonging to youth, job
opportunities for the wife, and demands on the time of the father. . . . Even
more disturbing in its implications for human understanding and human
development is the rising incidence of offenses by family members against
each other. In the total population these crimes are small in number, but
they are symptoms of a lack of human understanding within family life.
(11:3–4)

Other writers have stated that the family has remained a much more stable unit than is indicated in some current literature. These writers believe that family members still find their primary source of needed love and security through their relationships with one another even though individuals range far from home in search of satisfaction to their needs. For most Americans, the family is a life-long tie that is more intimate than other relationships, and for children the family continues to be the center of learning, socialization, and security. Havighurst and Neugarten state that change has not removed these functions from the family.

> Despite the historical changes and loss of some of its functions, the family has lost none of its importance as the primary socializing agency in the life of the child. It is the individual's first and most influential social system and provides him with his most influential social training situations. (5:150)

Investigators are in general agreement that the family continues to exert a most significant influence on children during their early formative years. "In shaping the early and continuing values, aspirations, achievement and behavior of the child, the family is without equal" (2:148). The degree of success a child realizes in school and beyond is dependent to a large extent upon factors that relate to the socioeconomic status of the family. The same applies to the child's educational and occupational aspirations. The expectations parents hold for children are closely related to family status and greatly influence achievement not only during the early years but on a continuing basis. The child's belief in his own ability stems from his self-concept as a family member.

School entry is too late to become concerned about human capacitation. What happens to the child during those early years prior to coming under the influence of formal education determines not only his school success but success in facing and coping with much of his later life. It may be debatable that this important time of life should take place in the conventional family unit, but it is becoming more and more evident that the chances of greatest life success come from early positive mother-child relationships. Pines, in reporting the Harvard Preschool Project, states that

> In this brief span of life, it appears, the mother's actions do more to determine her child's future competence than at any time before or after. She can turn him into a highly successful human being who—short of catastrophe—stands excellent chances of doing well at whatever he undertakes, or she can produce an intellectual and social failure who might be changed only with difficulty. Yet nobody warns her of the dangers of this period, nor of its promise. (12:63)

The greatest opportunity for both mother and child to find the love, warmth, security, and human relationships needed to ensure the child's maximum intellectual and social growth is to be found in an intimate family unit. The problem is to make the family unit an ideal developmental environment for every child during that formative time when his life's happiness hangs in the balance.

As a result of their research on "The Dangers of Early Schooling," Moore and Moore believe that the key to successful child development during the early childhood years is the parent-child relationship.

> . . . it seems clear that for a child of this age, development at home is far more important than development in school. And if the parents' acceptance of their role is a key factor in the child's development, then it makes a great deal more sense to educate the parents to fulfill their proper role than to hire teachers to do an inadequate job of trying to substitute for them. (9:61)

One of the objectives of careers education must be to bring to learners an understanding of the family unit and its contribution to the development and happiness of all its members. By the time future parents leave the public schools to face the responsibilities of their adult world, they should have a deep understanding of the influence their actions have on their children and an understanding of the relationship between family membership and the other careers. This is not to suggest that all adults must establish a family if they are to find personal fulfillment. It does suggest that young people need to possess these understandings in order to make valid decisions about seeking personal fulfillment.

The family unit should be more than an ideal place to rear children. It should be a very special sanctuary in the lives of its adult members. Within this sanctuary should be reached the ultimate in human living. Careers education should develop those skills of human communication and relationship that are basic to achieving these experiences of life. The ability to relate to others is not available "on call" when needed. Rather, it is developed from early childhood through adulthood. If the development of the ability to relate to others is to help children find fulfillment in family living as adults, the school should maintain a family-like organization and an atmosphere in which children can safely seek the most effective ways of establishing happy and productive relationships with their peers.

Minimum expectations should be set for family career development in the elementary school. By the time young learners leave the elementary school, they should have acquired knowledge of the importance of the family unit in all cultures. They should have had many opportunities to study the patterns of the family living of other peoples, in addition to engaging in a continuous examination of life in the American family. Acquired knowledge should include information about and an understanding of the influence the family has on the present and future success and happiness of children. Knowledge about the relationship the family career has to other careers should also be an expectation of careers education.

The school's responsibility to the family career in skill development is almost exclusively concerned with human relationships and communication skills, even though it is difficult to exclude certain "work" skills that carry over from home to school. Children should have developed those communication skills that are prerequisite to maintaining position in the family and to helping other family members find security within the unit. Included is the skill to explain through oral communication a situation, a condition, or a position. Also of considerable importance is the skill of listening; of accurate reception of the communications of other family members; and of a willingness to hear others "out."

Communication and human relationship are inseparable. They depend upon each other for consummation. The human relationship skills the school should expect to develop that relate to the family career are focused on functioning in small, somewhat intimate groups which involve the skills of communicating openly with peers. The ability to activate these skills in new and changing groups should be a part of the development of human relationships.

Attitudes are gained from the many and varied experiences individuals have. Elementary children preparing for the family career should be expected to gain from these experiences a positive attitude toward others generally and an attitude of trust toward those close to them. Attitudes are not easy to identify or assess but there should be some observable evidence of positive attitudes in the ways children relate to one another. Teachers should expect to observe an increase in behavior indicative of positive attitudes toward members of the school community and an acceptance of them.

Citizen Career

The school's efforts to help children become active participants in the processes of democratic living have generally been restricted to the forty-five or fifty minutes reserved each day for teaching social studies. Occasionally a citizenship club meeting has been thrown in to satisfy those supervisors who judge the worth of instruction by measuring quantitatively the coverage of the curriculum. This approach to citizenship instruction too often leaves children believing that if they perform the duties listed by the teachers to the satisfaction of the adults present in the school they will be good citizens. If they obey the rules set down by others, salute the flag, memorize the branches of government, know the names of their state's governor, members of Congress, and agree with the majority, they will meet adequately the school's expectations for citizenship behavior. To challenge the rules and want to participate in their formulation, inquire into the truth of a tradition, question an authority's decision, or organize a minority is to detract from institutional loyalty and lower the chances of receiving a passing mark in citizenship.

The methods employed in teaching have made a potentially interesting and practical area of learning disliked by a surprising number of children. Social studies is concerned with people and living. It is a twenty-four-hour-a-day, seven-days-a-week experience that should result in people living together more compatibly and more productively in terms of service to one another. What could be more exciting and relevant than that? And yet, the schools frequently are not developing desirable citizenship behavior. Murray and Brubaker agreed that the instructional approach traditionally followed in social studies has done little to change citizenship behavior.

> Most of the social studies traditionally taught in the schools have focused on historical accounts that emphasize unique events from the past. But too often these studies remain only interesting curiosities in the learner's life. They probably exert little or no influence on his present-day or future behavior as a citizen. (10:53)

It is, however, unfair to place all the blame for the problems of citizenship education exclusively on social studies. Its development is the responsibility of all areas of learning and all adults with whom children come in contact. Citizenship, like craftsmanship, is a way of life. Its responsibilities are not satisfied by going to the polls every few years to choose among names any more than demanding excellence of others qualifies one as a craftsman. Citizenship is not something that can be turned on in November by voting and turned off during the other eleven months. It is an on-going part of seeking and finding a satisfying life. It is the means of maintaining and improving our democratic way of living. It is continuous. It is a commonly shared career.

In elementary careers education, it is assumed that the best approach to help children become active citizens who make positive contributions to improving the quality of their living is to accept the condition that they are citizens of their world with the same rights and responsibilities of their counterparts in the adult world. The first requirement of this approach is acceptance of the existence of the child's world. Adults must accept the fact that children need to be included in making the decisions that affect their lives and that they will develop the skills and attitudes and acquire the knowledge required to direct their own destiny only if they are included.

In the school, involving children in processes of citizenship education should include the following steps:

1. Children should be included in setting the immediate goals of learning and living. They should have a citizen's responsibility to contribute ideas and ideals to the determination of what is important for them to learn.
2. Children must be full-fledged participating citizens of their school, charged with the responsibility for determining the learning and living conditions that will permit them to achieve their goals more effectively and efficiently.
3. Children should evaluate the success of their efforts to create a satisfying and productive environment.
4. Children should be expected to reconsider their goals and adjust the school environment in light of their evaluation.

For the young, being citizens finds meaning and reward only in their world. It is at this early age and within the limits of their environment that children must begin to develop appropriate citizenship behavior. Schools must be democratic institutions if children are to secure the skills of democratic citizenship. There is little possibility that, in an authoritarian atmosphere, children will gain the sensitivity and feeling for human relationships that are basic to discovering the benefits of democratic citizenship. In this regard, DeCecco states:

> In one sense they were asking for the same protection to exercise citizens' rights inside the school that they enjoyed outside the school. Why should it be any different? In fact, does not the school have the primary institutional responsibility to be a model democratic society? The Phi Delta Kappan national committee on human rights states this very well: "A democratic classroom must be one in which there is deep concern for the behaviors based on beliefs of this democratic society." The enormous gap between the democratic rhetoric of the school and its rigid control is about the most disenchanting hypocracy the students experience today. (3:170)

If school learning is to transfer to out-of-school citizenship performance, the patterns of school living must be more than a replication of existing community conditions. The school needs to be a model reflecting the highest ideals of democratic society. Children should discover for themselves the rewards of seeking truth and beauty in living by applying their combined strengths and talents to solving the problems of group living. Within the environment of the school, children need to experience the joy of helping and being helped by those group members who are different ethnically, socially, or intellectually, and who are more or less fortunate in terms of parental occupations. The nature of the model must help them come to the realization that democracy works best when each citizen meets his responsibility to the group and does his fair share of the common work.

Citizenship education must have a definite practicality about it. Learning the characteristics of a citizen or the accumulation of facts about citizenship cannot have the same impact on citizenship behavior as experiencing the rewards or suffering the consequences of personal and group decisions that are directly related to the matters of current living. Thayer and Levit point out that

> . . . today it is essential to have more than "knowledge" about these matters, in the sense of an exclusively intellectual preparation for citizenship. Young people require assistance in learning how to understand and get along with people, how to respond sensitively to and live creatively with their fellows. They need to acquire through practice in relatively simple situations the qualities and insights they must later apply in the solution of complex problems. . . .

> An "understanding of democracy" achieved by learning the words and routines representing the existing social norms is indeed a kind of animal conditioning that Hutchins and others condemn. So, also, is the development of sociable and healthy personalities, whether by benevolent manipulation or by coercion, which renders a person unable to inquire seriously and capably into what he and his society consider sociable and healthy. (13:45–46)

Increasing the practicality of citizenship education (and all education) by involving children in decisions concerning their own learning does not mean that they attack the problems of their society unaided or without guidance. It does not mean that teachers are excused from their responsibility to the learning processes nor that they cease to function as professional educators. It does mean that children are given the responsibility for identifying and dealing with the problems of group living that have the most importance. In meeting this responsibility, they should expect and receive adult assistance in developing the skills and acquiring the knowledge needed to design and activate the conditions of democratic living.

Children's thoughts and actions are focused on the present. It is doubtful that concentrating instruction on preparation for the future will do little more than consume the child's time. Learning must offer the possibility of meeting an immediate need if it is to reappear in the resolution of some future need. How permanent and functional learning becomes for children depends upon the variety of opportunities they have to apply it to situations of immediate concern to them. The quality of learning and the degree of skill gained in its application by each learner depends upon how carefully and thoroughly teachers plan for children to re-encounter the learning at ever-increasing levels of complexity and sophistication. Citizenship education, therefore, should be planned around the activities and experiences children design and initiate in their efforts to create a desirable classroom and school-living environment.

When children are included in the activities of identifying experiences that give importance to their learning, the teacher becomes more concerned with those instructional responsibilities that precede and follow active teaching than with "up-front" performance. Preparing to teach and judging how effective instruction has been in achieving objectives should be the two segments of an instructional-renewal cycle that make the active teaching segment successful. This cyclic arrangement for ensuring that instruction is appropriate, successful, and subject to continuous renewal is basic to all teaching in elementary careers education and is the means of gleaning from learner-identified activities all possible opportunities for children to gain the skills, attitudes, and the knowledge (under relevant circumstances) that have been identified as "basic" in elementary education. The obvious difference between this and the traditional approach is that children gain the knowledge, develop the attitudes, and acquire the skills needed to reach objectives that have immediate importance to them. It is a process, for example, of becoming a participating citizen; for only if each member participates as a citizen can the group achieve the goals they seek. Only through such an experience will individuals have the opportunity to internalize the human feelings that accompany rewarded citizenship behavior. When this happens, that behavior will reappear at later times.

It would be impossible to identify here all the knowledge that children should be expected to acquire as part of their citizenship education. Most knowledge is significant over a period of time in making decisions related to performance as a citizen but the social sciences come immediately to mind as important sources of information. Many children are rebellious toward the study of or the teaching of history, but they need to have an appreciation of the humanitarian ideals upon which this nation was founded. They need to know the principles that form the backbone of our way of life and how these principles were determined, if they are to perpetuate and improve our form of democracy. The need for this kind of knowledge has never been a secret. The task has been to get it to "take" with children in a manner that helps them make decisions that consistently indicate they possess knowledge of American ideals and accept the citizen behavior they stand for.

Important, too, is knowledge of the economic nature of our society. To establish a reasonable balance between their material wants and environmental and human concerns when they are adults, children must understand the cause and effect relationship that exists in an industrial society such as ours. An understanding of the repercussions of major adjustments or changes in the economy is prerequisite to making intelligent economic decisions in both the public and private sectors.

Closely allied to knowledge of the national economy is knowledge of personal economics. The knowledge base that supports profitable management of personal living and effective performance of the consumer role should be initiated in the elementary school. Citizens' personal economic circumstances greatly influence how they make political decisions and select leaders. Those who have the knowledge needed to deal adequately with the economics of their private lives are more apt to approach the decisions of public concern in an objective manner.

Part of this knowledge comes from the literature of the disciplines that has been adjusted to use in the elementary school and part of it comes from experience. The instructional secret is to blend the former with the latter in real citizenship experiences that can benefit from "book learning." Teachers must provide opportunities for students to apply their knowledge to situations that are real and important to them.

In addition to acquiring knowledge which is important to being an aware citizen, competency in the citizen career for elementary children should include proficiency in several skill areas of which human relationship and intellectual skills are of greatest importance. Citizenship is a career requiring skill in making both individual and group decisions based on concern for others and on reason. The effectiveness of making citizenship decisions that are intended to improve human conditions and relationships is dependent upon the ability to analyze existing conditions intellectually, identify needs, develop alternatives, and determine solutions. Decision making in a democracy requires that citizens think beyond self and objectively determine the effect their decisions will have on others both in the present and in the future. This requires a not so subtle interaction between cognitive processes and acquired attitudes toward people.

It is difficult to ferret out those attitudes that exert a particularly potent influence exclusively on citizenship behavior. It is difficult in fact to isolate any attitude and identify it as being of a specific species. But those attitudes that influence and control reactions to other humans and how their ethnic background, religious belief, or occupational preference should be considered in making decisions that affect quality of living are of maximum concern in preparing children for active citizenship performance. Also of concern to the school and closely associated with attitudes that deal with acceptance of others are those attitudes that children have toward their environment and other forms of life. The school's role in helping children acquire positive views and reactions to all factors that influence citizenship behavior is one of providing excellent models of adult performance in an environment of exemplary democracy in which students can test the adequacy of their attitudinal and value systems.

Vocational Career

The controversy among educators over career education has been centered around the vocational career. Many educators dismiss the career concept as no more than an attempt on the part of vocational educators to gain recognition on the educational scene. There are several reasons for this attitude. First, some people have taken the position that anyone lacking a college background is somehow unacceptable socially as well as occupationally. They have denied that part of the American dream that should lead us to believe that there are no untouchables in our land because of occupation, as well as race or creed. They have indicated by their behavior that dignity in the world of work is reserved for those whose occupations require schooling in an institution of higher learning. They have promoted the idea among the young that to provide for their families' needs by the sweat of their brow and the skill of their hands, regardless of the craftsmanship involved and the service rendered, is a social judgment handed down to those lacking in mental ability, personal drive, and maybe even the social graces. Sidney P. Marland, United States Commissioner of Education, states that

> We are so preoccupied with higher education that it has become a national fetish. High schools measure their success by the number of their graduates who go to college. People view vocational education as a great thing for the neighbor's kids.

Marland goes on to suggest that as a people, Americans have great need for

> *Getting over the idea that someone who goes to college is better than someone who does not,* enabling the American public to hold a first rate artisan who works with his hands in esteem as it does a liberal arts college graduate;
>
> *Increasing career education,* especially at the secondary and community college levels, because the nation has no place for the person who is not going to college and lacks a salable skill;
>
> *Giving minority children a chance to develop through education* and attacking the mystery of how to bring effective learning to the poor;
>
> *Closing out general education,* which offers nothing at the end of the line. (6:6)

Second, vocational education long has been labeled the Siberia of education by nonvocational educators. The academic stigma placed on vocational education has been supported by a social stigma placed on the products of vocational courses and schools. The social and economic rewards of an academic education have been blown out of proportion to the realities of human worth and dignity.

Third, public school educators have not worked together to meet all the needs of all the students. This attitude is readily apparent in our secondary schools where students who are judged not to be college material are placed into a variety of good and bad vocational courses, many of which offer little more than a place to hide the school's troublemakers and students in academic difficulty, and steals from the young life's most precious commodity—time. Regardless of the excellence of the courses, the students enrolled in them do not enjoy the same quality of school and community visability as those who have solved the problems of survival in the academic track.

Blame for this condition must be laid at the doorstep of both academic and vocational teachers. Neither has been accepting of the other or understanding of the purposes and possibilities of the other's program. Both, for reasons that belie the purposes of education, have exerted little or no effort to bring the strengths of their two areas together in patterns of instruction and experiences that would provide relevant education for all learners.

Public school vocational teachers often have been content to remain cloistered in their shops and drafting rooms. They have not made known the importance of their offerings to either their academic colleagues or their patrons. They have dulled any outside enthusiasm for their instructional potential by failing to note and promote the positive contribution they are capable of making to the education of *all* learners. They have done this by saying on the one hand that there is more to happy productive membership in our way of life than things vocational while on the other hand denying by their behavior that there are, in addition to vocations, other cultural imperatives.

In general, teachers in the academic areas have done little to resolve the vocational needs of their charges. They have rejected vigorously the idea that all education should make a more lasting contribution to the future vocational competence of the learners. They are smug in their self-imposed aloofness and satisfied with life in their world of transient facts. The content of their instruction seems not to possess possibilities for transfer to later encounters with vocational responsibilities.

Fourth, educators in high office are speaking and writing about career education from a very narrow understanding of the need for a total program or of the educational possibilities that exist within a career frame of reference. They are suggesting (some are insisting) that we give a vocational emphasis to the education of young children. Their idea of vocational emphasis is also unreasonably narrow. They are promoting in the name of career education what they call "awareness" of the world of work that is to be developed through field trips, resource people and "hands-on experiences" such as coping saw carpentry and cardboard construction. This "adds to" rather than takes advantage of an existing opportunity to give real meaning to each child's school life by creating an environment in which children can prepare for the world of work through the development of appropriate values, work attitudes, basic skills, and human relations through the process of solving problems that have immediate importance to them and doing the work necessary to establish desirable living conditions in their school community.

Finally, there are those in education who will use any excuse to avoid change regardless of how desirable or desperately needed that change may be. Part of this attitude comes from lack of understanding of the processes of change and, consequently, lack of acceptance of the inevitability of change. Some of the attitude is the result of individuals finding a comfort level of job performance so low that it erodes their professional dedication to children. At fault, too, is inadequate pre-service preparation which graduates teachers so unaware of the processes of education that they are incapable of recognizing the shortcomings of their own teaching.

Rather than accept this narrow view of the vocational career, elementary careers education seeks to develop the knowledge, skills, and attitudes that are basic to maximum performance in the vocational career and that contribute to success in the other life careers as well. The responsibility of the school to vocational development is not to provide a ready source of workers. It is to help individuals gain the ability to make accurate decisions about their vocational future and to help them acquire what is needed to make their decisions effective and rewarding. Meeting goal requirements in the vocational development of elementary school students is focused on assisting them in the acquisition of vocationally related knowledge, skills, and attitudes; and on providing them with experiences that have a direct influence on present and future vocational activities.

In a sense, all schooling has vocational implications and yet in the elementary school the intentional identification and instruction of knowledge related to vocational development generally has been avoided. Vocationally oriented knowledge appropriate for inclusion in elementary programs is of great variety. Mere awareness of the many vocations that have been listed probably contributes little to the learning of children but knowledge of the contribution made to our lives by members of many vocations has importance to vocational development. Knowledge of the dependent relationship that exists among vocations is important to children's gaining acceptance of members of all occupations, and understanding the role work plays in our culture should have some impact on vocational decision making.

Probably the most important knowledge to be gained at an early age is that vocations are comprised of people; not tools, machines, and factories. Children need to understand that teachers, carpenters, laborers, physicians, politicians, and workers of all sorts have needs, wants, desires, and dreams; and that in some way their vocation plays a role in whether needs of others are met or whether dreams come true. Children should have many opportunities to accumulate knowledge about people and life styles in order that they do not fall victims to the idea that once a vocation has been selected, life style is automatically determined. Youngsters must know that a fulfilled life is available to all, not a reward for being a member of a selected group of vocations.

The impossibility of knowing what vocations children of today will be entering or knowing what the entry level requirements will be makes it necessary for the public schools to prepare children to be adaptable and retrainable. Any attempt at specific training would be foolhardy. Bernard states that "adaptability and flexibility" are vocational skills.

> In today's rapidly changing technological world it would be more accurate to insert the word "initial" before the word occupation. . . . The typical worker will make six *major* job changes during his life. For a substantial portion of young people who are today in junior high school, the jobs they will perform do not yet exist. Adaptability and flexibility must be an important aspect of their vocational skill. (1:388)

The development of vocational skills in the elementary school is a broad undertaking that should not be limited to those "hands-on" experiences that permit the child to become acquainted with various tools and pieces of equipment. The skills that have broad vocational importance at this level have not been ignored in the past but neither have they been developed from a vocational frame of reference. The areas of proficiency of primary concern here are the physical skills, human relationship skills, and intellectual skills.

Elementary education seeks to provide the activities needed for children to develop physical skills commensurate with their physical potential. This obviously requires a great variety of activities all of which make some contribution to the development of the physical skills needed to enjoy vocational success. Credit must be given to physical education for making the greatest contribution to physical development, but credit for providing the variety of physical activities needed for developing vocationally related physical skills must go to all areas of learning. The fine muscular control required in many occupations is sometimes best developed in such areas as art and handwriting; and reading produces the eye control needed in most vocations, especially the technical ones. Science should provide opportunities for children to develop physical ability needed to manipulate both delicate and complex apparatus. Alert teachers will design activities in music, mathematics, and social studies that result in the development of physical skills with vocational significance.

At the point of departure from the elementary school, children should be confident of their physical performance and secure in their ability to meet the physical demands of their lives. How these demands are met in the school program determines, in part, how completely children develop physically. In order to meet the physical skills requirements of career education, the developmental nature of children must be considered. Teachers must include activities in their daily programs that will ensure, in terms of individual ability, sophistication in the use of psychomotor skills.

Human relationship skills do not lose their importance as people enter into the activities of their vocational careers. Job happiness for most workers develops from those working conditions determined and controlled by the nature of human associations that exist in their vocational world. Workers who receive little or no reward from their fellow workers find less satisfaction and are often less productive than those who are given recognition for their accomplishments by those who share an interest in their vocational efforts. The ability people have to establish positive working relationships with one another can influence productivity qualitatively and quantitatively as much as the level of vocational skill of the workers.

Securing, maintaining, and advancing a position in one's chosen vocation is as dependent upon human relationship skills as upon job competency. It is a tragic experience for many individuals who have devoted a period of their lives to preparing to enter a vocation to discover that employment eludes them because, regardless of how well qualified they may be, they appear insecure and incompetent when being interviewed. Perhaps even more tragic is the inability some skillful workers have to gain personal acceptance from other workers and as a consequence are removed from job after job.

Vocational success and security are also dependent upon the intellectual skills developed by each individual. The first step in ensuring job competency and happiness is the application of intellectual skills to the selection of a vocation. Because of an inability to become aware of personal capabilities and to identify and consider the consequences of their decisions, many people find themselves in jobs that are totally incompatible with their personal characteristics. Children should be helped to develop the intellectual skills needed to analyze and confront the reality of their natures, and to make decisions that are in agreement with their findings.

Children should be guided toward intellectual consideration of how continuous personal improvement in vocational competence can be achieved. This requires the acquisition of the skills needed to see beyond the "survival" requirement of the job and to determine the level of performance required to improve the quality of the product and the working conditions of the people concerned. It requires that individuals possess the ability to evaluate the adequacy of their current work skills and devise ways of improving them. For children to obtain these kinds of intellectual skills, "job opportunities" and guidance must be a natural part of the school program.

Workers must be capable of continuous learning if they are to meet the demands of a constantly changing technology. Laborers, tradesmen, and members of the professions face the common problem of having their means of securing a livelihood disappear through obsolescence or of having the vocational skills they possess lose their value because of the continual effort being directed toward increasing the efficiency and effectiveness in all areas of endeavor. The worker who is intellectually incapable of retraining for new vocational opportunities or advancing existing competencies to meet new vocational demands is apt to become an occupational derelict. Learning how to learn must therefore be a goal of elementary school careers education.

Attitudes related to vocations have their developmental beginnings in the early years of life. The attitudes parents have toward the worth of various vocations and the dignity associated with vocational membership is often reflected in their children. If the attitude persists, it will influence greatly the vocational decision-making process of the child. If the child sees all work as worthwhile and members of all vocations as worthy, the responsibility of instruction is eased considerably. If, however, the child accepts only a few vocations as worthy of consideration and values only those people who hold membership in the "elite" vocations, the school faces a difficult task.

Attitudes have an elusive quality that makes them difficult to teach and almost impossible to evaluate. Children arrive at school with firmly established attitudes. Within a single classroom, attitudes representing a variety of extremes may be identified. In this situation, the teacher may be forced to spend instructional time reconciling differences rather than helping children intellectually examine their reactions to others and to ideas. Such an examination is a necessary part of developing an attitude of acceptance that allows children to seek and to see good in all vocations and the values of membership in them.

Work attitudes are discussed at length in chapter 6. A brief introduction is appropriate at this point. Work related attitudes have some instructional advantage in that they can be somewhat specifically identified and defined. This encourages both direct and indirect instruction and permits students and teachers to judge results. Their nature also permits attitudes toward work to be rewarded intrinsically and extrinsically which generally improves the chances of permanent acquisition and further eases the strain on instruction.

Work attitudes differ from social and other attitudes and may, by strict definition, be more closely related to skills. They are treated as attitudes here because, when they become a permanent part of children's behavior, they are reflected in children's reactions to themselves and to those with whom they associate. These behaviors have to do with how children approach, attack, and complete a job, which influences the view others have of them which in turn influences the view they have of themselves. The attitudes being discussed are those that affect task identification, job responsibility, excellence of performance, task completion, and pride in accomplishment.

The attitudinal makeup of some people results in their being alert to work that needs to be done. They identify tasks in need of attention rather than ignoring them or being unaware of them. This is task identification and is an important part of any vocational performance.

Job responsibility is defined as not only doing a fair share of group-identified tasks but of doing the job when it needs to be done and in the manner that is required to meet the goals of the job.

Excellence of performance requires an attitude of dissatisfaction toward work that is performed at a level of quality below what an individual is capable of doing. It requires that workers know what level of performance their capabilities demand.

A job is not acceptable until it is complete. Task completion requires that a task be brought to a reasonable conclusion and that the quality of workmanship reflects maximum effort.

Workers should feel pride of accomplishment when the attitudes discussed above are brought to bear on a task. A spiral of improving attitudes and performance should result from experiencing pride of personal accomplishment.

Avocational Career

The puritan attitude toward work resulted as much from fear of idle hands as from fear of hunger. The way to avoid sin was to be too busy to partake of it. A generous view of what was sinful kept men, women, and children at hard labor much of the time. A contemporary view of what is sinful would undoubtedly be less restricting and more individually determined. Consequently, a work ethic directed at defeating the "old deluder" seems inappropriate to a technological society in which man is being freed from long hours of toil and in which people are being placed in a position of having time on their hands. And yet, one of the great problems facing American schools is helping individuals make wise use of this newfound freedom from labor. Our way of life can give individuals relief from their labors but the individual is sole judge of the wisest use to be made of any gain in nonvocational time. Herein lies the difficulty.

A view of education that permits the economic aspect of life to be the only acceptable curricular emphasis denies both the possibility of a future in which employment for economic gain will be on the decrease and the possibility that, for many, the means of human fulfillment cannot be found in monitarily rewarded work. This view also commits our education system to the perpetuation of a society that places more emphasis on the production of goods and the accumulation of wealth than on meeting the needs of all the people.

As the shift in the work-leisure relationship frees people to do something other than that which we have always held most important, we are apt to find ourselves caught up in a situation of discontinuity between our work values and a condition that we cannot avoid. Americans are not prepared for a world in which work is of less importance than leisure. According to Mather:

> Our society has prepared us for work, not leisure—and least of all, not for constructive leisure, for anything beyond beer, bowling, and boating. To be released suddenly from routine drudgeries is an appalling thing to happen to a man who has learned to master his job but not himself. (7:47)

Education then faces the task of preparing our children for life in a society in which the wise use of leisure time will be a necessity. It faces the problem of identifying the requirements of human happiness in a culture that has outgrown the need to consume people's lives in the production of required and desired goods. Green identifies the social as well as the education problem encountered in a situation of increased leisure time.

> For if leisure is free-time and if it is good to "find occupation for every moment," then the problem of leisure is to find "occupation" for free-time. The question then becomes, "What shall we do with this time?" "How shall it be filled?" "How shall we use it?" The problem involves how to use our free-time profitably, productively, and efficiently. The educational problem thereby receives its definition. It is the problem of educating people so that they will use their free-time profitably. (4:58)

The terms leisure, avocation, and vocation find different levels of acceptability in our society. In a period when leisure time and time spent on the job are in the process of seeking a new ratio, attention needs to be given to the implication each has to society, to education, and to the individual. Leisure by dictionary definition is "time free from work or duties and freedom provided by the cessation of activities." Consequently, such leisure is unacceptable to our puritanic idea of work. Margaret Mead sums up our working definition of leisure succinctly and understandably.

> Leisure, on the whole, is when people are doing what they want to do, doing something that is no human use to anyone but themselves. It does not apply to contributing to the community . . . it's very bad for unemployed youth to have, because they got it by flunking out of school. . . . Or take the theory of the leisure class who are using leisure to promote their own status. . . . However we look at it, we don't approve of leisure. (8:42)

Regardless of our attitude toward leisure, people need the opportunity, at appropriate times, to avoid activity if they so desire, or to engage in experiences that require justification only to themselves. Families and other close-knit groups can be destroyed by a member or members holding other members answerable for time and actions. So it is with children and leisure in the classroom. Children who are held accountable by teachers for their every minute and their every act soon learn that the best way to gain recognition and reward is to develop skill in determining what conduct will most please the teacher and then conform to that behavior. Creativity, imagination, and individuality suffer in such an atmosphere.

Children's needs to be left alone from time to time should be honored. Their desires occasionally to do something just because they want to should be respected as long as they are positive actions and as long as the welfare and activities of others are not interrupted. Young learners need to have the experience of finding a personal means of coping with the conditions of their lives through engaging at appropriate times in behavior that is uniquely their own. They need this kind of leisure time in the classroom.

The position taken here infers that leisure is partly a private experience that, if it is productive at all, produces primarily for self and not necessarily for others. In this aspect of leisure, self-concept is enhanced internally. Self-confidence is improved through discovery of ways of re-establishing equilibrium in times of stress and confusion. Providing opportunities for children to learn to make this use of leisure is a legitimate objective of instruction.

By strict definition, leisure and avocation differ in basic intent and because of this difference, "avocation" is used in the model of elementary school career education. As we move toward a leisure-oriented society in which more and more people are removed from the world of work, we must not lose sight of the need for individuals to feel a sense of accomplishment and usefulness. Neither can we forget that how we view ourselves is in part a perception of how others view us; and that others view us, in part, in terms of our achievements. Avocation implies a product through which we can gain a sense of personal value and that contributes to others' gaining a positive view of our worth.

The image that comes to mind when avocational product is being considered is something that can be seen, handled, and admired as an addition to the possessions of the producer. The inclination is to think of hobbies or subvocations that compliment the special abilities and interests of individuals. This view of avocation, though incomplete, is important to maintaining a feeling of usefulness. School activities seldom provide children with opportunities to produce an "honest" personal product; a product that is an expression of themselves and not a reflection of someone else. Part of the excitement of being a member of an educational community should be receiving gladly given assistance in pursuit of personal desires and interests. Teachers have not learned one of the secrets of dynamic teaching if they have not discovered that instruction in basic knowledge and skills is more effectively achieved when children are in search of goals that have special importance to them.

Giving vitality to instruction is justification enough for including avocational activities in the educational experience of children but there are other more long-range reasons why the avocational career needs to be a part of the school program. The early school years comprise a time for exploring many aspects of living. It is a time for attempting to find a harmonious combination of interests, activities, and purposes that will carry into and give consistency to future patterns of living. One of the factors sought in this compatible union is a means of finding a balance among the elements of living. With this in mind, children need to explore continually for an area of interest and activity that does not conflict with the activities of other life roles and yet adds a very special dimension of personal accomplishment to life style. School should be one of the appropriate settings in which to search out such an activity.

The school program should be so designed that learners come in active contact with a great variety of experiences; any one of which might be worthy of life-long investigation by an individual. The school day should be so ordered that any child can find time to become engrossed in the investigation of an interest that is of no particular concern to other classmates. Instruction should be individualized to the point of providing children with the guidance needed to acquire knowledge and develop skills that hold importance only to the achievement of private goals, and the methods of evaluation should encourage maximum performance in these classroom avocations.

Specifically what these avocational activities for children are or should be is difficult to state because they can be identified only by individuals. An activity must awaken an interest or create one if it is to be of value in helping a child search for a lasting avocational interest. This means that the school program must include activities that range from the active to the quiet, from the physical to the academic, and from the directed to the creative if each child is to have an opportunity to conduct a thorough search. For many children the selection of an avocation will not be made during the elementary school years, but without an opportunity to experience personal involvement with many suitable activities at this young age it is possible that a selection might never be made.

The results of avocational effort need not be a "hard" or visible product. During this time of decreasing work hours educators are faced with the tasks of preparing people to find personal satisfaction in devoting work-released time to service kinds of activities designed to benefit the lives of others in some way. Serving the young, the old, and the sick, seeking the means of resurrecting our environment, bringing back beauty to our world, and the many possible activities associated with these and other human services should receive emphasis at least equal to that given more measurable avocational products.

Unlike the other careers, the avocational career does not require the direct setting of minimum expectations of performance for elementary school children. Expecting each child to meet the conditions detailed in a set of objectives would defeat the purposes of avocational exploration. Children should be expected to participate in a variety of activities that might have future and lasting interest for them, but they should not be expected to engage in any activity to the point of boredom and rejection in order to appear in possession of an avocation.

The nature of the avocational career does not require the inclusion of specific knowledge in the school program. Knowledge acquisition requirements beyond that associated with on-going learning experiences does not become an instructional issue until after a child has demonstrated a continuing interest in an activity. At that time an opportunity for the individual to gain knowledge related to the identified area of interest should be available. Providing children with the materials, equipment, and instruction required to perpetuate and advance knowledge in a unique interest should be an important aspect of the pre-instructional activities of the teacher.

Skills related to avocations are often so unique and so foreign to traditional school programs that it is difficult to prepare in advance for their development. Children should have the assistance they need to develop the skills required to meet successfully the demands of maximum performance in their avocational pursuits. Such assistance must be available at the time the skill is needed if deterioration of interest is to be avoided. This may require recruiting people from the community who have special skills and are willing to work with children either in the school setting or in an out-of-school location that is more conducive to the development of the needed skill. This arrangement also permits children to become acquainted with workers under the more ideal conditions found in a helping relationship.

The pursuit of avocational interests loses none of its importance because of the inclusion of permeating influences in the elementary careers education model. Aesthetics, spiritual and moral values, and physical well-being are as much a part of the avocational career as any other career. It is possible that these influences are advanced as much or more through avocational and leisure interests and activities as through the seemingly more important careers.

Beauty and its appreciation is the reason many people make the avocational decisions they do. To capture on paper, canvas, or film the natural and man-made beauty that makes our world livable occupies the leisure hours of many individuals. The creation of new beauty through a myriad of approaches brings enjoyment to the nonvocational hours of creative people from all walks of life. Such activities can bring beauty into the lives of children and encourage them to look for beauty in everything and, hopefully, everyone about them.

Our values, spiritual and moral, are perhaps as much the result of the leisure experiences that have special meaning and excitement for us as the activities in which we must meet the expectations of others. Perhaps the personal honesty and integrity that should be a part of our relations with others and our productive activities are better acquired through seeking fulfillment in our avocations than in activities in which we have less personal control.

Physical well-being, competency, and security are the goals of more than a few avocational and leisure activities. Many Americans spend their "off-duty" time in activities that were selected to maintain and improve their physical capabilities. There is a relationship between how secure individuals feel toward their ability to perform physically and how they function in all activities, and so people who devote leisure time to physical maintenance and improvement also may be improving performance in other careers.

If there is a possibility that these relationships exist between leisure activities and other careers, then the avocational career is entitled to a position of importance in the elementary school program.

REFERENCES

1. Bernard, Harold W. *Human Development in Western Culture.* 3d ed. Boston: Allyn and Bacon, 1972.

2. Brembeck, Cole S. *Social Foundations of Education: A Cross-Cultural Approach.* New York: John Wiley, 1966.

3. DeCecco, John P. "Tired Feelings, New Life-Styles, and the Daily Liberation of Schools." *Phi Delta Kappan,* November 1971, pp. 168–71.

4. Green, Thomas F. *Work, Leisure, and the American Schools.* New York: Random House, 1968.

5. Havighurst, Robert J. and Bernice L. Neugarten. *Society and Education.* 3d ed. Boston: Allyn and Bacon, 1967.

6. Marland, Sidney P. Quoted in "Concern." The American Association of Colleges for Teacher Education, September 1971.

7. Mather, William G. "When Men and Machines Work Together." In *Automation, Education, and Human Values,* ed. William W. Brickman and Stanley Lehrer. New York: Crowell, 1966.

8. Mead, Margaret. "The Changing Cultural Patterns of Work and Leisure." In *Education in a Dynamic Society: A Contemporary Sourcebook,* ed. Dorothy Westby-Gibson. Reading, Mass.: Addison-Wesley, 1972.

9. Moore, Raymond S. and Denis R. Moore. "The Dangers of Early Schooling." *Harpers Magazine,* July 1972, pp. 58–62.

10. Murray, Thomas R. and Dale L. Brubaker. *Decisions in Teaching Elementary Social Studies.* Belmont, Calif.: Wadsworth, 1972.

11. Perkins, Hugh V. *Human Development and Learning.* Belmont, Calif.: Wadsworth, 1969.

12. Pines, Maya. "A Child's Mind Is Shaped Before Age 2." *Life,* December 17, 1971, pp. 63–68.

13. Thayer, V. T. and Martin Levit. *The Role of the School in American Society.* 2d ed. New York: Dodd-Mead, 1966.

Chapter 4 THE CAREERS OF CHILDREN PART II: LEARNING

Learning

Learning takes on a new meaning in schools dedicated to improving the quality of life rather than to merely "covering" a predetermined quantity of preselected materials. Learning in an atmosphere of living is concerned with assisting each individual to command the knowledge, master the skills, and develop the attitudes and values needed to find happiness under most conditions; see beauty in others and in surroundings; face adverse circumstances with a confidence that prevents personal destruction; and live, play, and work with others with feelings of trust and respect.

Educators need to accept learning as a necessity of total living that is not turned off and on as children enter and leave school. School learning needs to be so designed and provided for that it is a part of rather than an interruption of the continuous learning of living. Rather than living in two or more worlds, children should find that the benefits of learning in one setting are beneficial to living in other settings. The knowledge that is held valuable in the school should not lose its worth out of school; skills gained in the classroom should not have only classroom application; and attitudes developed to enable children to survive in the presence of teachers should not cause destruction in the presence of others.

What learning is and how it occurs have challenged the minds of investigators, theorists, and speculators for centuries. No satisfaction seems to be found in the agreed upon fact that humans do learn. Apparently, satisfaction will come for many only when the workings of the human mind can be predicted with accuracy and managed with efficiency. And then, of course, intellectual satisfaction will be frustrated by those who ask if what has been achieved is really learning.

Because of the multiplicity of explanations of learning and because of a general lack of knowledge of its occurrence, educators are often forced to consider the outcomes of learning rather than the processes required in achieving them. When the outcomes of learning are limited to collecting facts, the processes are restricted in both quantity and quality and school learning becomes inappropriate to living and preparing for life. The quality of learning may be determined by the number of applications children find for it in their activities and the variety of ways in which they apply it. It is to this practical union of the academic and the experiential that elementary school careers education is dedicated.

Elementary school careers education is process education that is simply but not narrowly defined. An attempt has been made to deal with all aspects of the model, including learning, in a manner that (1) does not "turn off" teachers and lay people at first contact; (2) permits local educators to adjust each factor to fit district philosophies and staff capabilities, and (3) discourages the kind of adult interference that makes the processes of learning so complicated that by the time they filter down to children, teachers cannot apply them and learners cannot benefit from them. To keep careers education manageable and learner-oriented, only five factors of learning have been identified as appropriate to the intent of the model. It is not denied that each factor can be highly complex in its development nor is this complexity ignored in the processes of careers education. It is also recognized that learners develop from "where they are" from existing human characteristics. Because of this belief, careers education is seen as an extension and continuation of those on-going learning processes that should result in the "fully functioning man" defined by Carl Rogers.

> He is able to experience all of his feelings, and is afraid of none of his feelings; he is his own sifter of evidence, but is open to evidence from all sources; he is completely engaged in the process of being and becoming himself, and thus discovers that he is soundly and realistically social; he lives completely in this moment, but learns that this is the soundest living for all time. He is a fully functioning organism, and because of the awareness of himself which flows freely in and through his experiences, he is a fully functioning person. (7:288)

Discussing each factor of learning in isolation is done as a matter of convenience with full understanding that it belies the nature of learning and the intent of careers education. Learning obviously does not occur in neat, identifiable, and discrete categories nor does a change in activity require that the learner shut off one "brand" of learning and turn on another. The purpose here is to deal with the second dimension of the model in a way that enhances the instructional view of the child and yet does not require the analysis of detailed learning theory. This is not to say that it is unnecessary for careers education teachers to have an understanding of learning theory. The opposite is true! Because of the "infused," "correlated," "integrated," "continuous," "translatable," and "transferable" nature of the objectives of learning that are the foundations of careers education, teachers must have considerable understanding of the field of learning.

The five factors of learning in order of importance to the child are:

Self-concept
Human Relationships
Intellectual Power
Continuous Learning
Knowledge Acquisition.

SELF-CONCEPT AND THE CAREERS

In careers education, development of a positive self image loses none of its importance and gains a real and fertile setting in which to prosper. A long-standing difficulty with much of traditional classroom teaching has been that feelings of adequacy acquired by children have been based on achievements that hold little or no importance to them. Accomplishments that have value only in the school setting may permit children to gain a view of self that can be easily shattered in the reality of the world beyond the school. When instruction is so designed and implemented that the intent of learner effort is to please the designer and implementer rather than develop the ability to solve problems related to improving the quality of life, the chances that this shattering process will occur are greatly increased.

Teaching methods that apply instructional materials in the name of student control only find no place in careers education because of the potential they have for denying children the right to see themselves as they truly are and as they are capable of becoming. One of the strengths of elementary school careers education is found in the emphasis placed on helping each individual develop a positive self-concept in an honest instructional atmosphere and in an environment that is closely related to the community outside the school. For children to possess the personal confidence required to face sucessfully the matters of finding a satisfying place in their society, they must have opportunities to discover the approaches to living that hold the greatest reward for them. Elementary school careers education is designed to provide such opportunities for children.

The means of helping each child develop, maintain, and improve self-concept in careers education is found primarily in the quality of classroom human relationships and the perceived intent of instruction. The nature of the program, the kind and quantity of materials available, and the appropriateness of the physical environment contribute to the development of self-concept in a secondary way.

How children feel about themselves in the classroom and school is mainly determined by the teacher's ability to promote positive human relationships. Whether children have a feeling of being wanted and a sense of belonging depends first upon the ability of teachers to convey an attitude of genuine acceptance to each child. An open-arms policy must give individual meaning to the open-door policy. Children need a human "home base"; someone to turn to in times of confusion and distress; someone they can depend on to be always available and understanding; someone they do not have to impress.

Second, teachers must have the ability and desire to find a secure place for each child with the other children in the classroom. Teacher acceptance often is of less importance to children than peer acceptance. Teachers who either fail to promote happy productive human relationships among their children or who deny such relationships among their children or who deny such relationships by requiring full attention on themselves are denying children a full opportunity to learn. It is just possible that, when the conditions of happiness and productivity permeate the classroom, children will become better teachers of children than are adults.

Third, all school personnel should have the ability and the desire to help all children feel a sense of membership in the school setting. Certificated personnel are professionally responsible for the total development, including self-concept, of all children in the school, not just those in their classrooms. Noncertificated staff should give evidence prior to employment of their belief in the worth and dignity of children. There should be no blind spots in positive human relationships as children move about the school in pursuit of a complete education.

The human relationship requirements of promoting self-concept are not unique to elementary careers education. They have always been requisites of good teaching. The unique contribution that careers education makes to the achievement of these essentials of learning is found in the teacher-student and student-student relationships that must be established and maintained in order for children to meet individual and program objectives in the various careers. The emphasis of the program is on learning to establish quality classroom and school living conditions and living under the conditions set. In pursuit of quality living, agreements are negotiated; common tasks are identified and completed; evaluations are made; human rewards are given and received; individuals are permitted by the group to pursue private interests; and teachers are involved in and held responsible for the success of all activities. In this arrangement of group effort and individual importance, opportunities abound for children to discover who they are and build on what they discover. Great are the professional rewards that come to the teacher who has the vision to see these opportunities and the competency to take full instructional advantage of them in developing the self-concept of young learners.

An extension of the alliance between human relationships and self-concept is evident in how children perceive the intent of the teacher and of instruction. Learning is probably more dependent upon how children *perceive* the intent of the teacher than on what the teacher actually intended. Caught up in the difference is how children perceive their importance to the teacher. Their perception of their importance influences how they feel about themselves, which in turn influences classroom performance.

When, for example, the intent of instruction, as interpreted by children, is to require them to memorize bits of information, and when teachers reward children on the basis of their success in doing this, they seek teacher approval by conforming to their perception of what is required to be "good" in the eyes of the teacher. The importance given to the memorized bits of information is related more to the gaining of teacher acceptance than to the more legitimate reasons for acquiring information. The result is that children are forced to deal in negative human relationships which is to say that they base the establishment of human relationships on false premises and, in the process, they are apt to develop less than positive attitudes toward the acquisition of knowledge. Self-concept built upon such shaky foundations is doomed to eventual collapse. There is an element of instructional (and professional) dishonesty present when this is permitted to happen to children.

In order for children to feel a sense of security in a wide variety of situations, teachers need to help them gain a positive view of themselves in an atmosphere that is focused on human and academic integrity. This means that teachers must have a clear understanding of the use of subject matter as a vehicle for giving the skills and attitudes of human relationships functional permanence in the lives of children. This understanding must reflect in how teachers approach instruction and, hopefully, in the intent of their effort as perceived by children.

Setting goals that are important and understood by children is part of the process of creating an atmosphere in which children can experience the benefits of the true helping relationship that is the key to instructional success in elementary school careers education. Careers education is goal-oriented in its attempts to bring balance to the academic-experience relationship. Teacher success, therefore, is dependent upon ability to plan and implement instruction in a way that "puts it all together" for children; in a way that fuses all aspects of the program and permits children to enjoy immediate rewards from learning as teachers guide them toward the long-range objectives of education. In this careers education arrangement, children and teachers should have positive feelings about themselves and toward others in the classroom family. Each should be able to interpret accurately and accept the intent of the other.

How children view their worth and how they feel about themselves greatly influences their acceptance or rejection of others. McDonald agrees that a child's view of self influences his attitude toward others.

> If a child sees himself as friendly, he is likely to behave in ways consistent with this self-image. He may say, for example, "I will get along in this group because I like people." In so behaving, he obtains need satisfactions, such as love and approval, from other people. But if experience tends to contradict his image of himself, the whole behavior sequence that has led to need satisfaction is threatened. (5:436)

The relationship between self-concept and performance must be a prime consideration in the design of school programs including elementary school careers education. When children view themselves as failures, they will indeed fail. Happily, when they view themselves as capable of being successful, they will succeed. Each child must have a successful experience each day. When the experience holds personal importance to the learner the success will be real and the resulting rewards will be worth striving for at some future time. When the experience results in failure, it may not be attempted again. If failure is allowed to continue, the entire life of the child may reflect failure. Noar agrees that failure in school can have damaging consequences in later life.

> Evidence is increasing that failing in school does in fact make people inadequate for living and working successfully. Teachers are therefore obliged to help pupils to avoid failure which kills effort, creates a negative self-image, increases anxiety and may lead to physical, emotional or mental illness (even suicide), all of which block learning. (6:96)

HUMAN RELATIONSHIPS AND THE CAREERS

The quality of human relationships children encounter in the classroom, school, home, and community determines in large part the happiness and success they find in the activities and experiences of learning. Children benefit from an atmosphere of positive human relationships in at least two ways. First, their personal lives and their attitudes toward learning are enhanced in an environment that encourages discussion of their successes and failures. In such a setting, they find freedom to experiment with many alternative routes to learning and discover how to convert failure to success. Second, open communication as a part of human relationships involves more than teachers and children. When all members of the community openly contribute to the education program, children find themselves living in a world of continuous learning. They discover that learning gained in one world has application in the other worlds of childhood.

This matter of human relationships between the in-school and out-of-school worlds of children goes beyond the immediate learnings of children. The establishment of positive human relationships among all people concerned with the education of the young has long been necessary to the success of educational programs. More than a few school systems have lost the support of the public because of lack of skill or effort or both in bringing the public into beneficial contact with the schools. Only when the problems of human communications have been resolved among all those concerned with public education will children reap maximum rewards from their education.

The quality of human relationships in the home is usually beyond the direct influence of the school. The school can be given little credit or blame for the relationships that exist among the members of most families. Attempts to make adjustments in the family life of children are constantly being made by teachers and other school workers. Some of these efforts are made on behalf of the human rights of the child. Too often they are directed at improving the academic performance of the child with no apparent regard for the need to provide for the physical child, the social child, and the emotional child before placing academic demands on the intellectual child.

If children are to experience fulfilled living commensurate with their level of growth and development, the schools must take the lead in creating a home-school relationship based on mutual concern for children. Elementary school careers education encourages the development of this relationship and in turn benefits from it:

1. Careers education considers the influence each career has on the development of human relationship skills. Awareness and development of these skills at the elementary level are centered as much around family roles, family citizenship, and family recreation as around the family as an economic unit.

2. Parents, as vital contributors to careers education both at home and in the school, are encouraged to join their children in the examination of the many facets of the several careers. How successfully children and parents are brought together in this relationship and how much it influences family living depends in part upon how carefully and thoroughly school personnel have established lines of communication with the home.

3. The success of the instructional program in elementary school careers education is partly judged in terms of the success realized by

each child in the development of human relations skills. The degree of success realized by each child in employing such skills to influence relationships among other family members is highly individual. Success will be most visible when today's children demonstrate their humanness in establishing warm and open interaction among the members of their families.

For many children there undoubtedly is a positive relationship between their ability to establish the human relationships needed to maintain self-image in the school and their success in gaining needed recognition in the home and community. The methods employed successfully outside the school will be tried in the school regardless of their acceptability or lack of it. The school has the happy task of helping those children who have discovered positive ways of gaining acceptance become more positive in their associations with others. The school must also accept the not so happy responsibility of helping other children discover acceptable methods of becoming wanted and contributing members of the group.

The quality of human relationships within the school and classroom should be less speculative than in other areas of childhood living. The only acceptable goal is for *each* child, including minority and disadvantaged children, to gain the skills, attitudes, and values needed to find acceptance, security and the motivation to perform maximally. Each individual should also be capable of accepting and providing security and motivation to others. In elementary school careers education, meeting this goal is prerequisite to meeting the goals related to gaining academic skills and functional knowledge.

The patterns of bringing children together in the school should be arrived at carefully to ensure that each child has many opportunities, with teacher guidance when needed, to discover appropriate ways to find happiness and personal effectiveness in varying social situations and under differing conditions. Grouping practices that require children to remain with others of their own "kind" for long periods of time contribute little to the development of human relationship skills and may even damage the personal security needed to feel comfortable in new and changing group activities. Any classroom organization that results in children continually seeing themselves and being seen by others as less capable and less acceptable than peers has no place in programs such as elementary school careers education in which self and relationships among people are believed to be basic to achievement of all worthwhile goals and objectives.

Classroom grouping patterns that promote positive human relations provide opportunities for children to experience membership in changing groups that recognize individual strengths more often than weaknesses. These groups need to be created primarily to permit children to pursue the group goals they have set for themselves as part of their efforts to improve the quality of classroom living through application of their ever-increasing abilities in each of the careers. Children with strengths in needed areas are given leadership and instructional roles in this approach to grouping. Each child, when ready and as often as possible, is given responsibility to use special competencies to advance the work of the group. Consequently, every child experiences intra-group relations from the point of view of leader, teacher, follower, and learner.

Small group situations in which the teacher assumes primary responsibility for direction should be temporary and planned to overcome specific difficulties that are hampering the children's progress toward career and academic goals and to evaluate student growth and achievement. Groups of this nature are called together by the teacher to resolve a problem that is common to each student in the group and should be dissolved as soon as the members have gained the level of competency required to be successful members of a current activity group. The human relationships emphasis in this kind of grouping is basically one in which the teacher can further establish a "helping intent" with each learner. Such groups help children learn how to seek and benefit from teacher assistance in dealing with problems of all kinds.

Each activity, experience, grouping arrangement, and instructional approach should be designed to enhance the creation of a family atmosphere in the classroom. Behaviors characteristic of such an atmosphere include support of each member by other members, acceptance of each child by the other children, help offered by individuals when others need help, approval given when approval is warranted, and positive criticism given when required. In addition, difficulties that occur between individuals are resolved by open discussion between the parties involved. The teacher often serves as a mediator but never as the judge and jury in these matters of human adjustments in the classroom.

One of the major problems of human relationship faced by American schools is how to integrate public education so that children from racially different backgrounds and children from disadvantaged homes can find acceptance. It is no compliment to our schools or to our belief in the American dream that there are boys and girls in this country who are treated as "untouchables." Accepting all of them into the schools and classrooms because they are children would be a magnificent first step but it would not be nearly enough. The kind of acceptance needed is a human to human (not an institution to human) relationship that radiates a feeling of being wanted. All children regardless of origin or background should be able to believe that there is something of benefit for them in the schools, and that the experience of schooling will help them find success in all the careers. This feeling of human acceptance and of being wanted comes not from institutional policy but from the kind of human relationships that children encounter in the educational setting. Harold Howe II identifies two changes needed to bring children of all races and backgrounds together beneficially in the schools:

> How then can we change schooling more fundamentally than by bringing together children of different races and backgrounds? The first requirement is a transition from competition to cooperation as the dominant mode of the school; the second is the alteration this shift in values will imply in the authority and human relationships within the school. (3:20)

Human relationships in the classroom and school are centered around the development of self-concept and solving the problems of group living. How individuals view themselves is to a large degree the result of human relationships. Self-concept influences and is influenced by human interactions encountered in all situations, including solving the problems of children living together in careers education programs. Success in each of the careers, in school and out of school, is as dependent upon the ability to maintain positive relationships with others as it is on the career competencies of individuals.

INTELLECTUAL POWER AND THE CAREERS

The terms "intellectual" and "power" have negative connotations for many and, consequently, it was with some reservations that the two words were brought together as one of the factors of learning in the elementary school careers education model. Intellectual and intellectualism have been abused in a variety of ways that generally imply impracticality, nonproductivity, and incapability for significant accomplishment. Being intellectual is seen by more than a few educators as being completely opposite to the generally held view of "career." And when "power," with all its nonhumanistic implications, is added to "intellectual" it seems totally unacceptable to give the united terms third billing in the list of learning factors. Perhaps the more personal possibilities of performance existing in the union of the terms made it appealing.

Cognitive processes, higher level thought processes, thinking skills, and the many other systems and processes that have been discussed in connection with the mental development of children are all a part of intellectual power but individually and collectively they do not seem to possess the essence of intellectual power.

The application of the intellect to classroom problems that are concerned typically with gaining a hold on subject matter sufficient to last through the next examination provides for little reappearance of the problem-solving skills involved or of the information around which the problem was constructed. Intellectual power is meant to be a lasting force in the lives of learners. It is intended to provide for those who possess it the ability to determine right from wrong in all situations, identify humane from nonhumane behavior, solve all personal problems, make decisions that enhance self-concept and advance the human condition, improve one's performance in all the careers, become involved in the lives of others in ways that give human meaning to their existence, and make learning a continuous way of life. Somehow the usual "schoolish" attempts at manipulating the elements of the cognitive domain fall short of what is being searched for in careers education under the heading "Intellectual Power."

The activities and learning experiences and the instruction that activates them are the keys to the successful accomplishment of school objectives. When activities and experiences are confined to desks and chairs and limited to subject-centered curricula, and when instruction is a dispensing process, intellectual development is severely restricted. For intellectual power to become the means of guiding one's life, learning experiences should reflect the nature, needs, and interests of the children concerned. Providing for these experiences also presents opportunities for children to gain intellectual power.

The involvement of children in the processes of setting goals for group living and their involvement in the identification of experiences appropriate to achieving these goals demands intellectual involvement in their own education. Such involvement requires that they arrive at an appreciation of the worth and dignity of each member of the classroom group, and that they gain the ability to recognize the needs and interests of each individual in their design for quality school living. Intellectual power begins to emerge when the identification and acquisition of the skills required to perform the tasks associated with the learning experiences are added to the intellectual requirements placed on the children.

The old adage that "experience is the best teacher" and that "there is no substitute for learning by doing" would seem to be complimentary to the idea of careers education. Whether this is true depends upon the relationship "experiences" and "doing" have to the intent of intellectual power. If the result of learning through experience is, for example, learning to perform a task by repeating it time after time as it has always been done without thought being given to creating ways to more efficiently use human effort and to improve the quality of the service or product, then it is foreign to the intent of intellectual power. If, however, experiences are proving grounds where the processes of continuous learning can be improved as individuals apply their intellectual abilities to improving both the process and the product of their effort, the intent of intellectual power has been honored. The kinds of experiences children have in school must contribute to the development of these thought processes. Taba states that:

... The effectiveness with which an individual thinks depends largely on the kinds of 'thinking experiences' he has had. Unguided these experiences may or may not result in productive models of thought. The task of instruction is to provide systematic training in thinking and to help students acquire cognitive skills which are necessary for thinking autonomously and productively. (8:87)

The need for individuals to be able to think autonomously as suggested by Taba is an important element of intellectual power. An obligation of the school is to move the child toward ever-increasing levels of maturity— toward the gaining of independence. The ability to make intellectually competent decisions related to family, citizenship, vocation, and avocation is part of autonomous thought and part but not all of responsible independence. Independency with responsibility means that decision making must frequently move beyond exclusive concern for how the outcomes of decision making will affect personal goals. How others will be affected by the decision must also be considered and it is here that the affective quality of intellectual power becomes important to advancing the human nature of the decision maker.

Intellectual power is intended to be more than the ability to meet the cognitive expectations of the school. In order for this to become a reality, schools must have expectations for learners that go beyond the cognitive domain and deal with the affective needs of students. According to Weinstein and Fantini, this need is not part of today's educational program.

> Today cognitive processes and content are riding the peak of the educational wave. Cognitive development is equated with mastery of instructionally prescribed content, with "understanding of" or "knowledge of" a variety of *academic* subjects, rather than understanding or knowledge of how these subjects can serve the needs of the students. The entire machinery of the school, including its reward system, reflects this stance; grades, promotion, recognition, and so on are based on the degree of mastery of the cognitive. (9:26)

In each of the careers children need to be able to set goals compatible to their desires, make decisions that are related to designing the best personal approaches to achieving the goals, know when the goals have been reached and what adjustments must be made in them for future improvements, and do all of this without losing sight of the rights and feelings of others. This requires considerable intellectual power. Joyce describes the school setting in which this intellectual power can develop.

> *It is possible for school faculties, working together to develop societies of school children who have the ability to organize themselves, to work together, and whose norms encourage intellectual pursuit. Teams of teachers, work-*

ing together, could develop strategies for developing such school societies that would make questions of "discipline" and "control" seem almost absurd. (4:18)

CONTINUOUS LEARNING AND THE CAREERS

Equipping children to be life-long learners is a prerequisite to maximum performance in the careers. Ensuring that children do learn how to learn and make continuous learning a way of living requires teachers who understand how learning occurs, who are capable of creating classroom environments conducive to functional learning, and who are alert to the uniqueness of learning patterns of each boy and girl. Requisite too is an instructional approach that is process-oriented and child-centered rather than academically-centered. A curriculum that reflects a here and now concern for the nature of young learners is also needed; and the learning experiences that flow out of the union of these factors should be relevant, important to children, and have counterparts in the out-of-school world if learning to learn is to be a fulfilled objective of the school program.

Teachers have almost exclusive control of the learning (or lack of learning) that occurs in the classroom. Expensive and exotic educational materials, innovated programs, and luxurious physical surroundings have little learning value in the absence of concerned, dedicated, and competent teachers. Learning how to learn is an important instructional objective only if the teacher makes it important. Teacher behavior in the presence of children determines in the main the attitude students will have toward school-centered learning.

It should be the professional nature of teachers to promote learning and learning how to learn by being desirable models of learners who continuously advance thier knowledge and their competency. They should be more learners than teachers in their work with children and rise to the challenge of new learning with an infectious enthusiasm. The ability to learn in ways other than from textbooks should be demonstrated by teachers as they go about the business of helping children discover how to become continuous learners. If teachers could be totally competent in meeting their responsibility to guide children toward autonomous thinking and independent learning, they might reach the ultimate level of professional accomplishment— they might work themselves out of jobs with given groups of children.

Teachers should, by their classroom behavior, give evidence of the rewards of being continuous learners who have applied their learning skills to achieving happiness and success in the various life careers. Teachers are only human and like all humans they have their triumphs and their failures but, if they are to help children seek the good life, their goals of living must be real and humanly oriented and their triumphs should greatly outnumber their failures. It never has been and never will be acceptable elementary methodology to tell children, "Don't do as I do, do as I tell you to do."

Whether children actually become capable of continuous learning may depend as much on how they relate to the human qualities of their teachers as on the more professional characteristics. Neither is indispensable, but learning is enhanced in an atmosphere of mutual trust that removes fear from the learning scene. Teachers, perhaps more than any professional group, must come through to their clients as real, honest, and trustworthy human beings who can be depended upon to give sympathetic help when it is needed. Successful learning in elementary school careers education, and all good education, is dependent upon the quality of the relationship the teacher is able to establish with the learner.

The instructional approach in elementary school careers education is dictated by the nature, interests, and needs of the learner. It is individualized in terms of the child's learning characteristics, personal expectations and desires, and the deficiencies that inhibit success in each of the careers. It does not pattern children's learning, routinize their existence, or measure their worth by their likeness to others or their developmental similarity to norms. Appropriate careers education instruction frees children to be who they are and helps them become who they want to be.

Instruction in elementary school careers education is based on the idea that the learning required for school success does not occur in the absence of some kind of structure. Structure in this sense is seen as a concern of individualization in which the role of teaching is to help each child discover and perfect the structure for learning that offers the greatest personal productivity. Finding this structure and developing it into an efficient means of gaining the rewards of capacitation is the key to learning how to learn and to becoming a continuous learner.

This instruction differs from what is usually labeled individualized instruction in that structure is individual and developed rather than general and imposed. Instead of constructing systems and programs into which all children are "plugged" and from which they cannot escape until they "plop" out thinking very much like all other "plop-outs," careers education instruction attempts not to lose sight of the uniqueness or the educational rights of each learner. Children are human and are therefore individually different from other humans in their motivational requirements for learning, as well as in how learning actually takes place. For this reason, each child is entitled to an equal opportunity to receive maximum benefits from school experiences, and instruction must be directed at discovering how to learn rather than at discovering how much content can be covered.

Individualization in its purest form requires not only tailor-made instruction and learning materials for each child but a curriculum that is constructed around the interests, needs, personal goals, and patterns of learning of individuals. This level of personalization of educational programming may not be possible or desirable but if children are to find the excitement in learning that is necessary to become life-long learners, the curriculum must appeal to boys and girls in several ways. First, curriculum must be appropriate to the general developmental and interest levels of the children concerned. Children cannot be expected to develop personal learning patterns that have a lasting quality if they encounter only learning experiences and content that is below them, beyond them, or unappealing to them. Second, the school program should provide the flexibility needed for children to pursue personal interests without damaging their social or academic position with peers and teachers. Development in each of the careers is a highly personal experience that requires exploration and experimentation activities that are designed to extend and improve the learning patterns of each child.

Third, curriculum should be developed around the careers in a way that ensures that learning acquired in school will have value, on a continuing basis, to the solution of problems in out-of-school living. Children should not have to "rediscover the wheel" each time they encounter a new set of circumstances. Learning skills should replace guessing and at least some of the trial and error approaches to seeking answers to their problems. The processes of continuous learning should give them the means of mentally making ties between past experiences and present conditions so that development in the careers is continually on the advance. Learning how to learn is more than a child's exercise; it is a means of making present and future living a satisfying experience.

KNOWLEDGE ACQUISITION AND THE CAREERS

The belief that the acquisition of knowledge is an honored objective of education is being eroded by the misinterpretation of several existing conditions and circumstances. First, the so called "knowledge explosion" has frustrated and complicated the problems of acquiring knowledge. For many, the rapid expansion of knowledge has provided the arguments needed to justify abandonment of knowledge acquisition as a significant goal of education. It is argued that knowledge is no longer manageable in the classroom because it is not possible for any one person to know all there is to know about even a small segment of a discipline, and because it is beyond human capacity to keep up with the rate of knowledge expansion in any area. Bernard's description of how rapidly this expansion is occuring seems to add support to such a position:

> Knowledge is growing so rapidly that it doubles in shorter and shorter periods of time. It has been estimated that if all man's recorded knowledge could have been compressed into one book up to the year one—itself an

accumulation of thousands of years of experience—it would have taken until 1750 to double that knowledge. But knowledge doubled again by 1900 (only 150 years as compared to the previous 1750 years). The next doubling—to eight volumes—required only fifty years, to 1950. Another doubling to sixteen volumes, would have taken until 1960 (ten years). And another doubling occurred in the next seven years—to 1967—when thirty-two volumes would be required. It has been estimated that ninety percent of all scientists who have ever lived are still alive. (1:465)

This is evidence of our ever-increasing ability to question and to arrive at appropriate answers, but it is not evidence that a decreasing importance should be given to knowledge acquisition as a necessary function of the school.

Second, instruction that equates the accumulation of isolated and irrelevant facts and the memorization of subject matter with the acquisition of knowledge has been so thoroughly damned (and rightly so) that it has become almost professionally unsafe to recognize facts, subject matter, and knowledge as necessary ingredients of all education programs. In the view of many educators and critics, for anyone to give importance to facts, subject matter, and knowledge is to demonstrate a greater concern for content than for children. In truth, children must be the focal point of any acceptable educational program but to deny the basic importance of the acquisition of knowledge in the education of children is to deny an understanding of the educative process. Elementary careers education is based on the premise that the level of preformance in the life careers is significantly influenced by how sophisticated each learner becomes in the pursuit of knowledge and truth. Instruction and knowledge are inseparable in careers education for instruction must be based on knowledge and directed toward its acquisition.

Third, a negative attitude toward the value of facts, subject matter, and knowledge has developed because of the way they are taught. Learners have not always been in possession of needed knowledge as a result of having been taught and of having met the requirements of the school. Too often the concentration of facts and subject matter has not resulted in the acquisition of any knowledge at all.

The problem is to find a means of identifying knowledge that will make a difference in the lives of children and an educational model constructed around experiences that stimulate the permanent acquisition of the identified knowledge. The experiences must be real and relevant, and the knowledge must have value in as many different experiences as possible. Such a relationship between knowledge and experiences, it is believed, exists in the careers education model.

The experiences that children have within the careers program are designed in part to promote the gaining of knowledge through learning to be decision makers and problem solvers. The effectiveness of decision-making and problem-solving processes is dependent upon the knowledge the individual has of the circumstances that created the need for a decision or a solution. The more that is known the more alternatives can be considered and the greater is the probability of arriving at a satisfactory outcome. Developing decision-making and problem-solving skills includes acquiring an extensive body of knowledge and knowledge of how to acquire new knowledge as it is needed.

Happiness, as well as success in the careers, is dependent upon an individual's ability to make value judgments. A relationship between values and knowledge is important to the development of a personal set of values that will enhance the ability to evaluate and make decisions consistent with personal beliefs. The quality and renewal of these beliefs are related to the amount and the importance of the knowledge they are based on. This relationship is supported by Cummings:

> Only with knowledge can we evaluate properly. Better values may then be said to be the result of increased knowledge. So it follows that the more knowledge an individual has of the real world, the better he is able to form value judgments in keeping with reality and the saner will be his behavior in respect to the real world about him. One might even go so far as to say that education is a prerequisite for sanity. (2:148)

Lack of knowledge inhibits progress in the development of careers skills and attitudes. Instruction must provide children with the knowledge basic to achieving careers objectives during the school years and the means of gaining the knowledge needed to experience careers success during the years after formal education has been concluded. Implied is the need for all children to gain mastery of a body of knowledge that is basic to understanding the cultural significance of each career; the importance of each career in our society and its survival; the affective, cognitive, and psychomotor skills needed in each career; and the consequences of incomplete or inadequate preparation for careers performance. This foundational body of knowledge as identified in elementary careers education is derived from the disciplines, professions and occupations, from the community and the home, and from the learners themselves.

Curricular Areas
and the Careers

Volumes have been written about content and instructional methods in each of the subject areas usually included in the elementary school curriculum. Elementary educators and specialists in the disciplines have prepared statements describing how best to teach children what is most worthwhile in each of the subject areas. Curriculum specialists have attempted to incorporate their own ideas with those of the authorities in the various fields in arriving at definitions of curricular content. In spite of all this effort, teachers make the final determination of what young learners are confronted with in the classroom.

The end result of all this adult curriculum activity has been that a majority of schools in the nation have subject-centered programs that impose on children daily fifty-minute periods of fact-mongering in each of the subjects. This separate subject organization does little to bring quality learning to children and does a great deal toward giving them false educational values. Rather than evaluating the worth of their learning experiences or the importance school learning has to the solution of problems in other environments, children are often led to judge the value of learning in terms of their ability to recall facts and earn grades.

One of the primary reasons for organizing the elementary curriculum around an interdisciplinary careers model is to give importance only to learning that reflects a high degree of professional integrity. Educational programs that have professional integrity hold children in the position of primary professional concern and manipulate all other factors of the learning environment, including subject areas, to help each child gain physical, social, emotional, and intellectual independence. The attempt to organize curriculum around the factors of living and learning rather than around subject matter is an attempt to take full advantage of the content and character of each discipline in the solution of the day-to-day problems encountered in seeking a satisfying life and to avoid giving an unreal importance to instruction that denies the true value of subject matter.

The careers education model proposed here does not add a new area to the elementary school curriculum. Existing curricular areas are adjusted to meet new goals and new questions are asked in seeking the most effective and efficient ways of achieving careers education objectives. "How can I employ art as a means of improving a child's self-concept as a family member?" replaces the more familiar, "What cute idea can I come up with for art this week?" "How can social studies be brought into the learning experiences of children so as to advance their intellectual power as citizens?" takes precedence over the usual, "How many pages in the social studies text must I cover this week if I am to get through the book by the end of the term?" And, "How can language arts instruction be used to improve citizenship performance and patterns of classroom living?" overrules the lesson plan notation, "Have the red group do the next five pages (31–34) in the language arts workbook."

The curriculum organization, instructional methodologies, and materials selection that result from seeking correct answers to these kinds of questions give the subject areas a realistic relationship to the entire school program.

The search for appropriate answers should result in the development of subject matter identification procedures that are directed at selecting that content which can be most appropriately employed as a vehicle by which the more important and more lasting outcomes of education can be realized. Implementation of these processes results in the identification of curricular content that offers the greatest assistance to children in their development of careers skills and attitudes. In determining what content is most worth teaching in careers education, each of the disciplines should be carefully examined for those concepts, principles, structures, investigative techniques, and knowledges that can make the greatest contribution to helping children become skillful and attitudinally positive members of their society.

We are inclined to forget that in the end, what is *actually* learned is controlled by children for they accept and reject curricular and instructional efforts on the basis of what is of most interest and importance to them. In forgetting this, we also forget to include children in the process of determining what an appropriate curriculum should include. Somewhere beyond the grey area that exists between the curriculum prescribed by adults and the curriculum accepted by children lies a curricular region that should be inhabited primarily by children. Beyond the foundational curriculum identified by various kinds of professional educators there should be a curriculum based on the interests and concerns of children as identified by them in the classroom. Beyond the concern for the inclusion of the various subjects in the curriculum should be a concern for making the program an acceptable and sometimes exciting experience for those for whom the school exists.

There are two interrelated factors to be considered in identifying and implementing this "action" curriculum of children. First, there are group interests and concerns to be recognized and included. Many of the objectives of elementary careers education can be met only when children work together in groups to solve problems that have special importance to them as they go about the business of making the classroom an ideal place to spend part of their childhood. The curricular content of this aspect of the program is the learner-identified tasks that are necessary to creating the living atmosphere defined by the children. The fact that these tasks may not be easily classified under a single subject area should increase rather than decrease their importance as part of the curriculum because they become the interdisciplinary "glue" that is so often missing in school programs.

Second, each child needs his personal interests and requirements accepted as a legitimate part of the total curriculum. Personalization of educational programs should mean that there are many opportunities for individuals to engage in learning experiences that are either personally identified or designed by others with the child's personal interests and needs in mind, or both. Personalized activities should be related to the child's performance in the careers rather than to subject areas even though the interest expressed or identified appears to be subject-centered. This is not intended to deny a child the right to pursue a subject interest that is not a part of the regular curriculum. It is intended to be an instructional suggestion to encourage children to use what is being examined as a private interest to achieve personal goals in the careers because of the greater permanence such application gives to all learning.

Permeating Influences and the Careers

One of the difficulties encountered in developing educational models and designing educational programs is that the model or program more often than not emerges as a collection of parts rather than as a unified whole. Implementation too often results in giving each part instructional autonomy with no attempt being made to establish learning relationships among them. Models and programs constructed around the various disciplines seem to automatically result in subjects being taught in isolation from other subjects. Frequently, teachers emphasize the subject they have special interest or preparation in and deemphasize the subjects in which they are weak. The result is an out of balance instructional program that fails to provide children with a total educational experience.

Consequently, there is concern that in the careers education model, instruction will concentrate on either the subjects or the careers rather than on providing children with a unified interdisciplinary learning experience that provides for development in all factors of the model. There is fear that one of the careers will be given greater importance than others or that one will be totally ignored, rendering the model useless in its attempt to help each child explore all factors of life style. The great concern, of course, is that unless this fragmentation of program is totally avoided, children are apt to fail to develop a high quality of learning that permits them to apply their knowledge and skills to the solution of a wide variety of problems.

Within the model, these concerns and fears are faced by building interrelationships among the various factors and by providing for the inclusion of certain influences that permeate the entire model. All factors of the model can be considered permeating influences in the sense that instruction must provide for the appearance and frequent reappearance of the knowledge, skills, and attitudes developed in each of the cells. This instructional requirement, if met, will cause the deterioration of the lines between the cells and eventual unification of all aspects of the learning experience.

To further ensure that children experience a unity of learning experiences, aesthetics, spiritual values, moral values, and physical development have been included as means of bonding the cells of the model into a relevant and meaningful unit. It is intended that these "Permeating Influences" be considered in planning each instructional activity and that there is consistency in the manner in which these factors are made a part of each learning day.

Instructional integrity is vital in creating the setting in which children can experiment with and establish value systems that direct all aspects of their living. That which is found to be worth valuing in one situation should maintain its value in most situations. Learning activities that fail to provide for this continuity need to be reconstructed to permit learners to develop value systems that give them security and consistent behavior.

Inclusion of the permeating influences in the instructional day calls for pre-instructional activities that seek and devise opportunities for children to encounter beauty in all their activities, encounter situations that require valuing and making value judgments, and participate in activities that develop physical confidence and competence. Instructional activities involve implementing the planned activities in a way that beauty, values, and physical well-being are made a part of gaining knowledge, skills, and attitudes. Of course, in the lives of children, these cannot be separated but teacher behavior that gives undue importance and unreal rewards to a single aspect of instruction will warp the view children gain of the value of their education. Postinstructional activities should include evaluations of student reaction, teacher performance, appropriateness and quality of learning experience. This evaluation should be based on how each individual reacts to the permeating influences in each situation and the influence they had on total performance. It is difficult not to "telegraph the punch" of teacher expectations to children and reward them when they see beauty where the teacher sees it, express the same values the teacher holds important, and find enjoyment in the physical performance that impresses the teacher. But this has nothing to do with a child developing uniqueness, and independence and evaluation must be directed at individual performance in these areas.

A note of explanation is needed at this point. Including aesthetics and spiritual and moral values should not require explanation but perhaps the inclusion of physical development requires some justification. Careful consideration was given to providing adequately for the physical development of children. Because of the great influence the physical well-being of the child has on total development and because of the importance physical competence has to performing successfully in each learning experience, it was decided to deal with the problem in two ways. First, health and physical education was included as a usual curricular area with the hope that it would be given more than the usual emphasis on the developmental nature of the child. Second, it was included as a permeating influence as a means of guaranteeing that advantage would be taken of every learning experience to provide children with an opportunity to gain maximum physical development.

There are several alternative ways of dealing with the "Permeating Influences" other than the means employed in the model. The first and most unacceptable alternative would be to deny their importance and omit them. A second alternative would be to accept their importance but assume that teachers would provide for their development by including them in their daily lesson planning. This has not worked well in the past and there is little reason to believe that it will improve with age. Third, a career that includes these factors could be added to the model. This could be a satisfactory solution providing that instruction did not isolate it from the other careers. A fourth approach might be to list the permeating influences under each career and provide for them accordingly. The method developed here is intended to give these factors unusual coverage and importance in the expectation that they will become part of the lasting value of education.

REFERENCES

1. Bernard, Harold W. *Human Development in Western Culture.* Boston: Allyn and Bacon, 1970.

2. Cummings, Susan N. *Communications for Education.* Scranton: Intext, 1971.

3. Howe, Harold II. "Start With the Schools." *Saturday Review of Education,* March 1973, p. 20.

4. Joyce, Bruce R. *Alternative Models of Elementary Education.* Waltham, Mass.: Blaisdell, 1969.

5. McDonald, Frederick J. *Educational Psychology.* 2d ed. Belmont, Calif.: Wadsworth, 1965.

6. Noar, Gertrude. *Individualized Instruction: Every Child a Winner.* New York: John Wiley, 1972.

7. Rogers, Carl. *Freedom to Learn.* Columbus, Ohio: Charles E. Merrill, 1969.

8. Taba, Hilda. *Teacher's Handbook for Elementary Social Studies.* Palo Alto: Addison-Wesley, 1967.

9. Weinstein, Gerald and Mario D. Fantini. *Toward Humanistic Education: A Curriculum of Affect.* New York: Praeger, 1970.

Chapter 5 ACHIEVING PROGRAM SUCCESS

Introduction

The development of an educational model, as an isolated act, makes little difference in the lives of children. An educational model is of value to children only when it has been activated by adults who are dedicated to helping our young find fulfillment in a world they have helped to improve. Such dedication and help must be supported by expertise and resources in great variety and consequently must come from a variety of sources: professional education, parents, business, the community at large, and from the learners themselves. Program success depends upon the quality of the contributions made by individuals and groups from each of these sectors and how completely they solve the problems of establishing working relationships that result in improved education for the community's offspring.

Each segment of the community has an important and unique contribution to make to the success of careers education. Whether or not each contributes fully to its educational program depends upon whether it is brought into the activity and how the ability and desire to serve is continously renewed. This is true for both professional educators and lay people. This chapter is concerned with the preparation, selection, and renewal of teachers and with the identification, involvement, and support of community members participating in the program.

Preparation and Renewal
of Personnel

Learning is a unique human experience. In the school environment, the quality of learning is positively related to the quality of the human relationships children experience—the quality of the helping relationships that exist between children and teachers and among children. Whether education is an experience that results in positive human learning depends upon the ability of the school staff to create an atmosphere in which interpersonal communications are complete. Whether children enter the school each day with an eagerness to participate in the activities of learning depends upon the competency teachers have in establishing and maintaining a learning environment in which each child experiences acceptance and success. Whether children leave the school with the desire and ability to be life-long learners is determined by the attitude of the teachers toward learning. And whether children become self-sufficient adults who have compassion for other humans and concern for all living things is influenced greatly by the model set by their elementary school teachers.

In short, whether existing programs are changed enough for new educational goals to be reached is in the hands of classroom teachers. Teachers are in command of change and they will determine whether or not the ideals and ideas of elementary careers education will become a part of the learning experiences of children. Whether educational change occurs and whether the goals of elementary careers education are achieved is dependent upon the personal and professional characteristics, the nature of professional preparation, and the success of in-service renewal of teachers.

Educational ideals and ideas have little value unless they make a difference in the lives of children and in the quality of our living. The beliefs of too many of our educational thinkers appear only in the confining content of educational philosophy and psychology classes and have failed to enter the classroom world of children. There seems to be an impregnable barrier that historically has prevented the processes of change from replacing what "is" with what is needed. Katz, in his statements about the nature of our schools, states:

> . . . that certain characteristics of American education today were also characteristic nearly a century ago; it is, and was universal, tax supported, free, compulsory, bureaucratic, racist, and class-biased . . . I do not deny, or wish to imply that I deny, the introduction of important innovations —for instance, the kindergarten, vocational education, guidance, testing, and various new curricula to name a few. These have all made a difference, but they have not touched or altered the structural features I have outlined. (5:xix–xx)

Of greatest concern here is that in spite of the adoption of the listed innovations, the schools have remained "bureaucratic, racist, and class-biased." The problem is an inability on the part of educators to design, develop, or discover the means of implementing ideals and ideas that encourage full acceptance into the learning world of the school of all children on the grounds that they are human beings.

The barriers to educational change are found in people. Educational change will take place when people change and generally people will change when there is a chance for personal reward. When the rewards of change are social and professional position, personal recognition, group acceptance, monetary gain, fulfillment of commitment, or one of a host of other rewards, people will respond.

There are at least as many reasons for resisting change as there are for accepting and encouraging it. Humans seek stability in their lives and avoid any change that threatens existing conditions without visible rewards. Any change that threatens individual competence will be resisted as will changes that appear to lower or negatively alter the quality of personal living. Changes that oppose an individual's beliefs, values, and commitments will be viewed as unacceptable.

Part of the processes of change must be concentrated on preparing educational personnel to accept confidently and seek actively changes that will keep education current with other social changes. People who accept and seek change are those individuals who possess a high degree of self confidence and professional competence. In part, the attitude toward change is a personal quality, a matter of professional perparation, and a matter of professional maintenance.

PROFESSIONAL PREPARATION

The reasons for entering education are difficult to ascertain and the attitudes students possess when they enter teacher education institutions have not necessarily been a great concern to teacher educators. According to Leiberman, teachers come generally from the lower middle and lower classes and, "For most people who enter teaching, it represents a chance 'to get ahead in the world,' a chance to climb from the blue collar to the white collar class" (6:218). Leiberman goes on to state that "strong interest in children does not seem to be a particularly significant factor in the majority of decisions to become a teacher" (6:218). These statements were made in the 1950s and it is hoped that entry into teaching now is being made for more altruistic reasons. Certainly if programs as human-oriented and as child-centered as elementary school careers education are to be implemented successfully, teachers must be selected and admitted to preparation programs on the basis of their commitment to serve others and on their ability to meet the demands of a rigorous program of professional preparation.

The processes of selection and admission should be repeated at all levels of the teacher education program. There should be evidence throughout the program that individuals preparing to teach find life in the classroom exciting rather than dull; challenging rather than routine; and freeing rather than confining. This, of course, requires that a portion of the college requirement must be met through some kind of relationship with in-service teachers and children in regular school classrooms.

There are dangers present in teacher education programs that depend too heavily upon field programs to equip beginning teachers to assume classroom responsibility, and such an overbalance could be disastrous in elementary careers education. Dependence on field experience tends to inhibit change and perpetuate educational conditions as they are. The old cliché that "teachers teach as they were taught (or as they see teaching occur) rather than as they were taught to teach" has credence when education students are evaluated in terms of the similarity of their performances to the performances of their models and to the expectations of their supervisors.

Successful instruction in elementary careers education requires a different vision of children in the learning environment than the image normally resulting from twelve to sixteen years of exposure to public school and college classrooms. "While teachers-to-be start out with a relative accurate picture of what most teachers do, what most teachers do is not what they *should* be doing" (8:471). Instructional planning for careers education cannot be based on images of children confined within the physical limits of the classroom and school, stationed behind institutional equipment, and engaged in activities that have little relationship to their out-of-school environment. Children should expand their learning environment into the community and beyond, use the materials and equipment that have counterparts beyond the confines of the school, and participate in experiences and activities that relate in many ways to all aspects of their existence.

Other means of creating the vision must be provided, because the ingredients of such an image are generally not available in the field segment of teacher education programs. The use of simulated environments offers an opportunity for students to make decisions, solve problems, and test various teacher behaviors. Laboratory situations in which students can experimentally create a variety of learning environments and in which they can learn to identify and prepare the materials needed to resolve specific career development and general learning difficulties of individuals is another means of helping them move beyond current instruction and toward what instruction should be. There are other means of directing the preparation of teachers toward new horizons and new ideas of how this can be accomplished will continue to be developed. The unavoidable requirement of these preparing experiences is to provide the basis for the continuous improvement of teaching and learning and to provide for the continual advancement of our profession.

It must be noted that simulated and laboratory experiences cannot supplant field involvement. There is great value in having education students join children and teachers in the activities of public school classrooms. There just is no substitute for working with children as part of the processes of gaining teaching skill. Only in the presence of children can the desire to teach be confirmed and only in association with children can sophisticated teacher behavior be developed. The ability to recognize problems and the observational skills needed to design ways of dealing with them are developed through continuous interaction with children. There is no textbook way of gaining the full significance of individual differences. Gaining an appreciation for the uniqueness of each child is not a vicarious experience.

From the careers point of view, the problem is not the desirability of field experience but the nature of that experience in relation to the requirements of instruction in careers education. The field setting does not usually provide opportunities for education students to become involved in the kinds of teacher and child activities that are characteristic of careers education and it is because of this shortcoming that experiential alternatives must be sought.

Education is, or should be, a scholarly profession. Intellectual confrontation and challenge must be central in teacher education if programs of teacher preparation are to prepare young people to teach in ways that are commensurate with the needs of children who will be living in the twenty-first century. This responsibility of teacher educators cannot be satisfied through field assignment of students or camouflaged behind a smoke screen of pedagogical courses and programs that fall short of meeting the central purpose of teacher education as identified by Silberman:

> The central task of teacher education, therefore, is to provide teachers with a sense of purpose, or, if you will, with a philosophy of education. This means developing teachers' ability and their desire to think seriously, deeply, and continuously about the purposes and consequences of what they do. . . . (8:472)

Commitment and purpose in education come from knowing and from feeling; from understanding people and their need to learn. It is important to understand our culture and the culture of others and how cultures are perpetuated and advanced through the education of the young. An understanding of the role of the individual in our society and of the role of the social and economic importance of the family is required. Gaining an awareness and understanding of the forces that influence and tend to control our way of life cannot be neglected. Needed, too, is a thorough understanding of the political nature of our country and world and of our political responsibilities to both. This knowledge and understanding are basic to making a life-long commitment to serving humanity through teaching children.

The knowledge and understanding required to make a total commitment to education must come in large part from learning experiences (not exclusively from the common variety of superficial beginning college courses that are usually required of education majors) in anthropology, art, economics, history, literature, music, political science, and the sciences. The intellectual involvement in these areas should be of sufficient depth to provide the learner with the knowledge (not transient facts) needed to understand where we have been, where we are, and whether the human race is worthy of survival. This knowledge should also provide *students of education* with an understanding of the importance of organizing learning in the elementary school around the life careers.

The interdisciplinary approach to both elementary education and teacher education further requires that college instructors in the various disciplines who teach education students have at least as much commitment to the education of children and youth as they do to their area of expertise. They must be able and anxious to help future teachers acquire the understanding of humanity and the mastery of subject matter needed to provide children with a truly comprehensive education.

Another important aspect of quality learning in these disciplines has to do with the content of instruction. In spite of rumors to the contrary, teachers (especially teachers of an integrated program such as elementary careers education) must have command of a substantial amount of subject matter. The quality and quantity of the subject matter teachers possess must also be greater than Goldhammer has observed it to be.

> ... it follows that the teacher must have mastery over the substantive content for which he is responsible. . . . Our earlier observation on contemporary knowledge suggests, however, how virtually impossible it is for the teacher to be such a master. . . . If the teacher cannot be, or is unlikely to be, a master of a broad or special knowledge, then of what does his mastery consist? Perforce, it consists of mastery over the material to be taught. The third grade teacher, consequently, if he is any kind of master at all, is bound to be a master of third grade knowledge; the seventh-grade teacher knows secondary school science; the tenth-grade civics teacher knows tenth-grade civics but not, necessarily, grownup political science, sociology, economics, or law. . . . Our observations on the curriculum suggest that, in large measure, he has mastered various caricatures of knowledge, make-believe disciplines consisting of fictitious and distorted facts, conscienceless omissions, archaic puritanical values, and other intellectual junk. (3:24)

If this statement is an accurate evaluation of the knowledge level of teachers, the need to adjust teacher education requirements is critical. The ability to teach is dependent upon the teacher's mastery of subject matter, for without mastery teachers will be unable to exploit content for all possible instructional opportunities.

Along with possessing knowledge beyond the third-grade level, teachers should have the experience of investigating at least one discipline (education is not considered a discipline here) in great enough depth to develop higher level thought processes than usually result from exposure to beginning and survey kinds of courses. A prime goal of education is to help children become competent thinkers and the success of students in careers education is dependent upon the ability to apply intellectual processes to the matters of living and learning in the classroom. It is believed that teachers must have experienced the trials as well as the excitement of in-depth learning if they are to guide children through similar experiences in the elementary school. The commitment and competency that results from this kind of intellectual activity is a necessary step in preparing to teach but it alone or in combination with field experience is not enough.

A third area of great concern in becoming a careers education teacher is the gaining of an understanding of the physical, social, emotional, and intellectual character of young learners. Teachers should not be permitted in classrooms until they have demonstrated an ability to recognize when children are developing, or failing to develop, in positive directions and at acceptable rates. In order to work with children, teachers must know the social acceptance, or lack of it, that each child feels in the classroom. Teachers must be aware of the human and physical environmental conditions that promote or inhibit learning and they must be able to identify emotional maladjustment whenever and wherever it occurs. Teaching is concerned with resolving the problems of children, and teaching by this definition can occur only when teachers are capable of recognizing when a problem exists. The only teacher behavior worse than that resulting from an ignorance of the nature of children is a "head-in-sand" behavior by teachers capable of problem identification.

Academic preparation appropriate to this segment of teacher preparation should be the study of human behavior in sufficient depth to bring about an understanding and acceptance of human individuality. This apparently requires more than the usual smattering of psychology and memorization of normative data. The level of expertise needed requires intellectual investigations in human growth and development, psychology, social psychology, and the other areas of human study, and concurrent study of and work with children in the classroom and community. This is needed to give functional meaning to the belief in individual differences we have so long only professed.

Helping students discover "how" to teach is still the good work for which schools of education exist. If education lacks "credibility on the campus" and if education majors lack "dignity in the dormitory" it is because, in the eyes of instructors and students in other departments, education does not meet the requirements for membership in higher education. Education may be too important an endeavor to want to be considered a part of this elite society, but if our profession is to survive, teaching must continue to require an extended period of preparation beyond public school graduation. This is true not because of the definition of a profession but because the education of our children demands that educational personnel be highly competent in a great variety of academic and experiential areas. This can best be accomplished on campuses where education has earned full acceptance as a legitimate and necessary area of advanced study.

Recognition of education as an honored field of study will depend upon how successful schools of education are in taking advantage of the characteristics of higher learning in bringing education students to a level of competence that enables them to (1) diagnose accurately the needs of individual learners, (2) prescribe the teacher behavior required to resolve the diagnosed need, and (3) evaluate present accomplishments, movement toward agreed upon goals, and the accuracy of the original diagnosis. To accomplish this, teacher education programs will have to be designed to graduate students who are in possession of the cognitive and affective skills needed to become involved intelligently and humanely in the life of a child.

Young people preparing to teach in elementary careers education programs need to be more concerned with learning how to establish classroom conditions that encourage positive human relationships and open communication than with accumulating a "methodological bag of tricks." A major part of creating such an atmosphere is being able to relate on a personal basis with each child. Buchanan refers to this ability as "affective expertise" and states that its development has not been a part of teacher preparation.

> The typical teacher preparation sequence includes a smattering of educational philosophy and history, an overview of one or several educational psychologies, a methods course which is often only a bag of tricks, and a student teaching experience, which may or may not allow the student to function fully as a teacher in the classroom to which he has been assigned. Nowhere in this sequence are the unique responsibilities of the teacher as an individual discussed.

> I believe the time has come to develop affective expertise. . . . Affective expertise means, first, the ability to reach a student as a fellow human being and, second, to feed subject matter into that relationship. . . . To both model and use affective techniques as a curriculum for a teacher education course is what I perceive as a revolutionary step toward change in the American school classroom. (1:615–16)

Another aspect of teacher preparation important to the education of all teachers and particularly those who will be implementing careers education is that "the best teacher is an excellent model." Instructors in schools of education need to be living examples of the behavior they advocate. They must be models of the instructional competence and humanness they expect their students to acquire and put to use. Contrary to the spirit of elementary careers education are instructors who find college and university employment the best means of financing and providing time to pursue avocational interests or who use college teaching as an excuse to pursue other academic interests. Such behavior is also contrary to the "model congruence" principle which suggests, in part, that teachers of teachers must be expert in their ability to inspire maximum future teacher performance in their students by performing maximally as teachers themselves.

Change in education seems more dependent upon the preparation of young people entering the profession than upon the willingness of those already teaching to adjust their teaching behavior.

PROFESSIONAL RENEWAL

How ideal it would be if teacher preparation programs not only provided individuals with entry level competencies but also provided them with built-in continuous renewal capabilities! It appears logical to assume that there is a positive relationship between how carefully and completely teacher education prepares individuals to enter the classroom and how capable education graduates are of benefiting from in-service opportunities for professional growth. It also seems reasonable to assume that teachers who are willing to participate in renewal opportunities and who are capable of benefiting from them should have available to them school-sponsored activities that offer opportunities for achieving personal and professional growth that results in improved learning opportunities for children in the classroom. Unfortunately, no matter how logical or reasonable they appear these are frequently false assumptions.

According to Misner, Schneider, and Keith, typical efforts to provide for the professional growth of in-service teachers includes such activities as

> ... teacher institutes; workshops; pre-school conferences; monthly grade level meetings; observation of lessons; intervisitations and excursions; lectures; or speakers; curriculum-development programs; development of resource units and courses of study; conferences with faculty, parents, and pupils; study groups; provision of professional reading materials; participation in public relations programs; attendance at professional meetings; extension classes or summer school courses; and provision for sabbatical leaves for travel or continuing education. (7:203)

The relationship between these activities and improved instruction is controlled by several factors, but the most important determiner of success is the attitude of the individual teacher toward the activity and any one of these may place a strain on the possibility of teachers finding them exciting and rewarding enough to benefit from them.

The professional growth of teachers is not an extraneous activity in elementary careers education. Teacher renewal takes on a more personal dimension and is an integral part of the program that philosophically and psychologically parallels student growth. All members of the school community are considered learners in need of assistance in acquiring the knowledge, gaining the skills, and developing the attitudes required to meet the demands of their responsibilities. Teaching and learning are continuous processes to which both teachers and students have an obligation and in which they both find personal rewards. For teachers, this part of the in-service program requires the existence of certain conditions.

First, it depends upon the presence or immediate availability of the needed assistance. Who provides that assistance—the principal, the consultant, an outside resource person, a fellow teacher, a community member, or a student—is of little consequence as long as the human conditions of teaching and learning are maintained and as long as the expertise required is on hand at the moment of greatest effectiveness.

Second, lines of interpersonal communications need to be established that are open enough to encourage teachers to request in-service help when it is needed and from anyone capable of giving it. This, of course, is in good keeping with that aspect of careers education that encourages children to establish the communications within the school and community that will permit them to seek from all sources the help they require to solve the problems of living in the classroom. Like their young charges, teachers should be evaluated on their ability to find and take advantage of appropriate resources, as well as their ability to solve personally the problems of learning.

Third, there needs to be a sense of community in the school—a sense of mutual and helpful concern for the success of the educational program as reflected in the learners. Jacobs describes this "spirit" as the "essence of being human and humane."

> The essence of being human is to be in charge of one's life—to assume responsibility for oneself, to be willing to renew and remake oneself on the basis of evidence that renewal and remaking are essential to one's well-being as an individual . . .
>
> The essence of being humane is the sensitivity and thoughtfulness afforded by one to another, not in a spirit of sentimentality or tolerance but rather in a spirit of honest sentiment and a willingness to work for a sense of community. To be humane is to recognize that one must contribute to the making of our world. (4:464)

Fourth, within this sense of community each teacher must feel a personal sense of security that diminishes the fear of failure and frees the individual to explore and experiment with new and hopefully better ways to work with children. This level of trust and security results when the rewards for facing and overcoming failure are similar to the rewards given for success. Gardner states that unless this condition exists, growth will not occur.

> We pay a heavy price for our fear of failure. It is a powerful obstacle to growth. It assures the progressive narrowing of the personality and prevents exploration and experimentation. There is no learning without some difficulty and fumbling. If you want to keep on learning, you must keep on risking failure—all your life. It's as simple as that. (2:17)

When these conditions have been met, the in-service growth of teachers will cease to be an instructional appendage. It becomes an integral part of the total educational program designed to help teachers become masters of their own professional destiny and shareholders in the educational enterprise. For this to occur, however, administrative support will be required in the form of: (1) providing released time to plan, initiate, and evaluate all aspects of the endeavor, (2) providing expert assistance in identifying major problems and in solving problems that require special expertise, (3) providing the funds needed to secure outside assistance when it is required, as well as other necessary instructional resources, and (4) acknowledging program success and teacher achievement.

Built into this plan for teacher renewal must be a means of overcoming the negative attitudes so frequently caused by many of the methods being used to evaluate the professional worth of teachers. Teachers need to develop, as a part of their integrated renewal program, a method of gaining "accountability" recognition for evidence of teacher self-evaluation. This will require that teachers develop a number of alternative techniques for evaluating their in-service performance and growth that are acceptable to the administration, and that they assume individual responsibility for implementing one or more of the techniques. Ideally, all of the alternatives should provide for continuous application and be concerned more with the immediate affairs of the classroom than with quantitative evidence of related behavior.

Like children's learning in careers education, the in-service education of teachers must have an immediate and beneficial result. Expending teachers' time and effort seeking solutions to problems that may or may not occur in the future will not permanently change adult behavior any more than emphasizing future living in education will alter the behavior of children. Renewal activities must concentrate on the solution of problems that have current importance to improving the effectiveness of the school, classroom, and educational program.

If they are to find interest and excitement in renewal activities and if the results of these activities are to have an immediate beneficial effect, teachers must play a significant role in identifying the in-service problems they are to attack. This not only gives teachers a sense of ownership and involvement, it also places the burden of responsibility for the nature and quality of their renewal program on them.

The use of the word "problem" in discussing teacher renewal programs does not mean to imply that in-service activities should move from "crisis to crisis" even though attempting to re-establish stability to an unstable situation is a necessary in-service activity. A problem, as the term is used here, is meant to include any circumstance or set of related circumstances that influence positively or negatively the quality of the education of the children receiving it. Problems worthy of inclusion in an in-service program could range from an individual teacher's attempting to find a more efficient way of performing a simple daily chore to a total group effort to reconstruct a major portion of the educational program in order to overcome current visible weaknesses in it. The important criteria to be employed in the identification of a problem for in-service consideration are: the relationship of the problem to the quality of classroom living of children, the immediate importance the solution has to the educational welfare of all concerned, the opportunities it offers for personal and professional growth of teachers, and the long-range benefits to be derived from its resolution.

There are two equally important, interrelated and inseparable tracks in this kind of renewal program. First, there is a personalized element in the program that is included to permit and encourage individual teachers to employ the resources of the school in dealing with the more personal aspects of renewal. It is included also to alert teachers to their responsibility for their own renewal. Part of being a professional is concerned with the intrinsically motivated acts of keeping abreast of new educational ideas and changing conditions, and continually being alert to areas of personal weaknesses and to ways of overcoming them. Another aspect of this individualization has to do with an extrinsic effort to prepare each teacher to perform successfully under changing conditions. Renewal efforts should include continuous motivation and assistance in advancing all areas of individual teacher competence. Teachers should be helped to prepare for the adoption of new programs, procedures, and materials without threat to their performance security.

Second, and to a degree dependent upon the success of the personalized part of the program, is staff involvement in improving the more global elements of the education of children. The initial and perhaps most difficult problem is finding a way to unify the staff into an effective and efficient problem-solving body capable of identifying and solving problems of group concern. Unification of effort is dependent upon the ability of the staff to develop a sense of purpose to guide and inspire them in their labors. This can occur when teachers seriously take for themselves the goals of humanism and democracy set for children in elementary careers education. Renewal is a full-time personal obligation of teachers. Like education itself, renewal requires continuous and intense concentration and effort. All who accept the responsibility of being teachers must also accept the challenge to seek ways continually of revitalizing self and of improving the model children emulate. Teachers must hold themselves accountable for extending the educational opportunity of all children and for improving the quality of student learning. Without an individual commitment to personal growth on the part of teachers, achieving the goals of elementary careers education is questionable, and education may not be able to assume a posture of readiness for facing the challenge of twenty-first-century living.

As a part of the renewal program, teachers need to remind themselves frequently that children do not suddenly and mysteriously gain mature independence. Gaining independence is a developmental process that requires time, patience, and all the instructional competence that can be mobilized through professional preparation and in-service education of teachers. The goal of all our efforts to improve ourselves and our ability to teach is to help each child become the compassionate and competent human we have so painstakingly described. Teachers should find reward in seeing this kind of growth in their children and be challenged to increased effort and improved performance when these traits are lacking. Renewal programs should help teachers experience these rewards and meet these challenges.

The success of elementary school careers education is dependent primarily on the quality of the instructional staff. Because careers education is community education, program success is also dependent on how congenially and effectively working relationships are established between school and community. The quality of this relationship will depend on how carefully plans are made to bring the various segments of the community into active involvement with the staff in all phases of program development and implementation. For this reason, it is of great importance to maintain the involvement principle and the cooperative spirit of careers education in planning for community participation in bringing about educational change.

The survival of careers education will depend upon implementation procedures that encourage all people concerned to accept positive change. A source of amazement to people outside the field of education is the number of apparently good educational ideas that have been publicized and how little they have altered the quality of the educational product. It is difficult for many people, including educators, to understand why potentially good programs disappear somewhere between the drawing board and the building area. Difficult, too, is explaining to lay people the processes of educational change that repeatedly filter out the new ideas and leave the old methods unscathed. Program designers should be challenged to seek more effective ways of assuring that solid educational programs arrive intact in the classroom, rather than being discouraged by the ineffectiveness of the processes of change.

The Community and Careers Education

Careers education is community education and its success depends not only on acceptance by the community but on the willingness of community members to participate in all phases of the program. Long-range effectiveness will depend on the manner in which community representatives are involved in designing and implementing the program. Continuous community involvement will depend greatly on the skill employed in identifying and organizing the initial groups and committees. Each segment of the community must feel included and fairly represented. Domination by any group or individual could be disastrous to keeping interest and involvement at a high level.

One aspect of organization that will influence the long-range effectiveness of community support is the approach employed in the identification of individuals to serve on the various groups and committees. Several factors need to be considered in making the selection process acceptable to the community. First, a temporary group representative of the community should be organized by the school leadership and charged with responsibility for conducting the initial identification activities. Second, democratic procedures should be developed and employed in the compilation of a list of community members from which final selection can be made. Third, criteria to guide the final selection should be written. Fourth, selection should be made and agreement to serve should be obtained from those selected. Fifth, assignments to the various committees should be made.

The identification of advisory groups and committees by title and charge requires careful organizational examination. There seems to be a tendency in school operation to appoint a new committee every time a new problem arises. To prevent the careers implementation organization from becoming a committee-bound administrative monster, adequate time and effort must be devoted to determining an optimum number of groups and committees needed to have an effective and efficient organization. This can be accomplished in part by preparing guidelines for accomplishing program development and implementation and from these determine division of labor and number of work groups. Also important is the preparation of statements of committee responsibility and authority and the development of a description of intercommittee relationships in terms of communications and flow of work. Helpful in keeping down the number of committees is the development of a procedure for assigning tasks that fall outside usual committee responsibilities.

In developing the operational organization, it is imperative to keep in mind that community trust and support will be influenced by the manner in which tasks are completed and progress achieved. Organizational provisions also need to be made for conducting a continuous survey of elementary careers education learning resources available in the community. All locations in the community into which the school program can be productively expanded and into which children will be welcomed need to be inventoried. Individuals with specialties required in the program who are willing to contribute to the learning of children in the school need to be identified and placed on the inventory. Procedures should be developed for keeping the inventory current both through evaluation of the instructional worth of locations and individuals, and by adding and deleting entries as the community population changes.

The School Staff and Implementation

Gaining staff support and creating teacher excitement for the program is also one of the necessary first steps in developing and implementing elementary careers education. They, along with the children, maintain the most complete and effective lines of communication with the community and without their support the program is in difficulty before it gets started.

The elementary school staff may be the most difficult group to convince that careers education is an improvement over what they are currently doing. The vocational education connotation that has been given to career education makes it appear to elementary teachers to be an inappropriate educational program for young children. Many of them also feel that they have been doing all the "awareness" activities that are needed and that careers education has nothing new to offer the elementary school curriculum. Whatever their feelings toward the program may be, without their approval and active support, the program will not be successful. For this reason extra effort must be made, through involving them in all phases of program development, to encourage teacher backing for careers education. It behooves careers education leaders to plan carefully for including elementary teachers in every step of the development implementation.

Involvement of school staff should be in the name of program development and improvement rather than a means of "selling" an already developed program. It has to be assumed that staff members have an important contribution to make to ensure a quality program and, if given the opportunity, they will provide a sense of reality to development and implementation activity. In view of this their responsibility at this stage of program development should be to keep the program instructionally feasible, in addition to sharing their ideas and knowledge about children and teaching. This requires a careful evaluation of every proposed step and addition to the program for its degree of relevance in terms of classroom instruction. This also places a responsibility on teachers to accept or reject all or part of the program on the basis of objective data.

If careers education leaders do their job professionally and objectively, staff members should gain a genuine enthusiasm for being a part of the school and the new program. Teachers should be prepared to accept the program into the classrooms with a security that is derived from a sense of purpose, a sense of ownership and commitment, and from understanding what is expected of them as the new program becomes operational. To assure that teachers do in fact understand their role in careers education, attempts have been made to define the role and responsibilities of teachers as a part of the implementation effort. The Mississippi State Department of Education made one such attempt to identify the responsibilities of teachers in a vocationally oriented career program:

RESPONSIBILITIES OF THE TEACHER

1. Making every effort to understand the values and purposes of the program.
2. Cooperating with the administration and career staff in carrying out policies considered essential to the development of career education.
3. Exchanging information with colleagues that would be helpful in meeting the objectives of the program, and which would help students make a better personal, social, or education adjustment.
4. Observing pupils in various activities in and out of the classroom, noting their patterns of behavior in group situations and becoming aware of their interests, attitudes, values, work habits, etc.
5. Recording behavior which they feel is a significant indication of career choice to be filed for future reference during career counseling.
6. Instilling proper attitudes toward work and study.
7. Giving pupils individual assistance in making desirable social adjustments.
8. Becoming aware of careers related to the subject areas taught.
9. Creating methods of relating to and incorporating career information into subjects taught.
10. Creating in the students an awareness of possible careers in which they will be involved in the future.
11. Cooperating with occupational orientation teachers in planning career related activities to be implemented in the classroom.

12. Providing information that will help students to make appropriate educational and vocational choices.

13. Communicating to the occupational orientation teacher how the concepts and objectives of the career-centered curriculum are being carried out.

14. Referring students who show definite interests in specific career areas to the occupational orientation teacher and/or counselor for additional information. (9:17)

Guidelines for Program Development and Implementation

Because of the community nature of elementary careers education, a discussion of its implementation cannot be limited to an examination of the processes required to place a completely developed program into operation in the classroom. Implementation begins with the birth of an idea. How the idea is advanced and how its support program is developed are basic to implementation. Achieving success in the program can be enhanced by constructing guidelines to direct the development and implementation of the careers education idea.

The careful preparation of guidelines for program development and implementation should be an early step in bringing together representatives from all interested groups. Ideally, participants should know something about careers education and have an initial excitement for it. In order to improve their ability to contribute to guideline development, a continual effort should be made to advance their knowledge of the possibilities of careers education. Information, of course, should be given to increase the effectiveness of participants rather than to promote private views of the program.

Several states and localities have developed guidelines for achieving implementation. These pick up the action at a point considerably beyond the birth of the idea and usually they are developed to gain support for an idea that has been rather completely developed. These generally include only major headings and activities and do not detail the methods of arriving at conclusions. A four-phase, ten-step outline for implementing a careers education program was developed under a U. S. Office of Education grant by the Maryland State Board of Education and presented in *Career Education: A Handbook for Implementation*. It is intended to be "general action steps for implementing career education" and does not pretend to deny the existence of "hundreds of detailed steps . . . required for most communities to implement programs of career education."

TEN ACTION STEPS FOR IMPLEMENTING
CAREER EDUCATION

Phase I

1. Organize the appropriate interactive network of interested individuals and groups.
2. Promote an understanding of the concepts of career education and establish appropriate educational objectives.

Phase II

3. Study the current educational system to determine the changes necessary to turn it into a true career education system.
4. Inventory and marshall all available resources.
5. Design the career education system most appropriate for your community.

Phase III

6. Gain the cooperation of all necessary organizations, institutions, and individuals.
7. Implement the system.
8. Build in an evaluative process to determine how well the system is working.

Phase IV

9. Create a feedback system to use evaluation findings to adapt and improve career education programs.
10. Make provisions for a program of maintenance to sustain early initiative and tie these activities into the interactive network. (10:69)

The Department of Education for the State of Nebraska developed a set of guidelines that differs in a few respects and offers another example of how a school might proceed in the implementation of career education:

GUIDELINES FOR THE IMPLEMENTATION OF
CAREER EDUCATION

The following steps may serve as a guide to administrators planning to initiate career education:

1. Organize a Career Education Advisory Committee.
2. Promote an understanding, within the Advisory Committee, of career education.
3. Establish goals and objectives for a local career education program.
4. Build a basic model for a career education program.
5. Analyze the present curriculum to identify elements of career education currently underway.

6. Develop a career education curriculum plan which will expand or build upon desirable career education elements already included in the instructional program.

7. Identify any modifications needed in materials, equipment, facilities, or personnel.

8. Determine what components can be implemented immediately. Establish a time line for implementation of the entire program.

9. Order any materials and equipment needed.

10. Conduct in-service training for the entire school staff and community persons who will assist with the program.

11. Implement the program.

12. Build in an evaluation system.

13. Provide follow-up assistance for teachers.

14. Make any needed revisions. (14:13)

Identifying Goals and Objectives

As the processes of careers education implementation continue, community members and educators will begin to assume different roles. A good example of this is in construction of goals and objectives for the program. In the beginning, both groups assume a joint responsibility for preparing goal statements that in general terms describe the program and the product. As the program matures educators assume responsibility for developing the more specific statements of objectives that influence instruction and form the basis for evaluation. Thus, the roles of the two groups become differentiated.

The joint statement should reflect agreement on the nature of the program and what it intends to achieve. The acceptability of the statement and the completeness of its content will be in proportion to the thoroughness of the process devised for accomplishing statement development. The process should begin with an examination of the approved school district philosophy and statement of objectives to ascertain whether the new program is in agreement with current school expectations. If a discrepancy exists between the old and the new philosophies and the community supports the new statement, the district statement will have to be rewritten. The district philosophy, as approved by the school and the community, is the key to continuity of thought in development activities and consistency of direction in implementation procedures. It must be well-organized, understandable, and acceptable in order to serve this purpose.

The perusal of career education literature from all sources, particularly that which is emerging from ongoing programs, is a prerequisite activity to writing goal statements. Care must be taken, however, to maintain the intent of the district philosophy and not be swayed by the easy availability of elaborately worded statements prepared by other people for other circumstances. An examination of programs from various parts of the country revealed a surprising similarity of goal statements. The children of each community are entitled to a program that reflects their needs and their community's uniqueness.

The inseparable activities of preparing the goal statement and securing its approval also require joint community-school effort. Writing general program goals and objectives should include the preparation of several drafts, and following each writing the statement should be reviewed and adjusted by the community and school groups. Each rewriting should bring the document closer to representing the community-school desires for the program and, consequently, closer to being approved. If the process is successful in providing for adequate community representation and if the writers are patient in their efforts to write a representative statement, the final draft may have approval even before the ink is dry.

Examples of goal statements are offered here only to give an idea of the results of some goal-writing efforts. They are concerned primarily with the vocational career but may be similar at least in form to goals for other careers. Some care was taken to select statements that are different. The first example was prepared by a group of "prominent educators from Guidance, Vocational Education, Curriculum, and various subject matter areas," who met in West Virginia to discuss, among other topics, "Identifying goals and objectives of Career Education." The final statement was published by the West Virginia Department of Education.

CAREER EDUCATION GOALS

The Career Education emphasis is directed toward:

1. Producing individuals able to understand and relate themselves both cognitively and affectively to their work.
2. Producing individuals motivated toward constructive work.
3. Producing individuals who have had exposure to the world of work vicariously, simulated and/or real, to the extent that they have some comprehension of the diversity and complexity of work alternatives both available and appropriate to them.
4. Producing individuals able to function in the performance of decision making and work adjustment processes.
5. Producing individuals who have the background necessary to enter their chosen career and to progress within that career or to change the direction of their career if necessary or desirable.
6. Producing individuals able to find and participate in meaningful work.
7. Producing individuals who see education as a continuing life process that is relevant to their life needs.

8. Producing individuals who contribute to and are rewarded by society.

9. Producing individuals who have had exposure to the world of education to the extent that they have some comprehension of the diversity and complexity of educational alternatives both available and appropriate to them. (16:3)

The second example is taken from "Teacher Guide for Increasing Vocational Awareness of Elementary School Children," prepared for use in the Pleasant Hill School District, Pleasant Hill, Oregon:

A program attuned to the vocational awareness of students extending from kindergarten to adult, should address itself to broader, more comprehensive objectives—not just informational services. These may be expressed in the following manner:

To provide students:

With a foundation for wholesome attitudes regarding the worth and the function of man's work in our society.

With an understanding of the world of work that would contribute in a constructive way to the development of each one's self-image as a productive member of society.

With an opportunity to develop a self-understanding as an awareness of their personal responsibility for making their own decisions.

With an opportunity to develop attitudes of respect and appreciation toward workers in all fields and in all levels of work.

With an understanding of their developing personal interests, attitudes, aptitudes, abilities, and skills as they relate to future career decisions.

With an understanding of the broad range of occupations open to them through education. (11:2–3)

The final example appeared in the Annual Report, Career Development Program, School District of the City of Pontiac, Pontiac, Michigan. The goals and objectives of the Pontiac Vocational Career Development Program follow.

Goals and objectives of the project

Goals:

1. To provide elementary and secondary students with a broad occupational orientation.

2. To provide students with work experience.

3. To provide students with specific training in job entry skills.

4. To provide students with intensive occupational guidance and counseling and initial job placement.

5. To provide for the contractor to carry on the program after Federal assistance is terminated.

Objectives:

1. To provide materials and information to teachers to be used in regular school program in the classroom.
2. To plan and conduct assemblies, career fairs, and field trips to further encourage students to explore careers.
3. To provide students to observe and talk to role models on the job and to schedule role models in the classroom to answer student questions on the World of Work.
4. To meet with parents to assist them in understanding the opportunities available to students in vocational training.
5. To coordinate the school program with community agency and group programs.
6. To study and revise the role of secondary counselors. (12:1)

Beyond this point, community involvement in the consideration of goals and objectives is centered on the continuous examination and revision of the prepared statement. In the spirit of the ideals of elementary careers education, the community must always be a part of the process of determining what the program is expected to accomplish. The organization for continuous review should grow out of the organization that was developed to prepare the original statement and should maintain the same level of community representation.

Writing the more specific goals of instruction and evaluation is an educator responsibility. The form that instructional goals and objectives takes is a local educational decision. Whether they are competency based, behaviorally stated, indicators of measurable outcomes, or representative of any of the other descriptive titles now in vogue is a matter for local education to resolve. The instructional objectives listed in the publications of the various programs are often more general than specific. The examples quoted here were selected because of their variety. The initial example was taken from "Tigard Career Education Program," which was prepared in the Tigard, Oregon community. The objectives listed were selected from the instructional objectives for the career awareness program.

Student Goals

Goal A Objective—Provide relevant learning experiences in CAP [Career Awareness Programs] through curriculum.

1. Student will locate and present descriptions of careers in their own community.

2. The student will be able to describe the career of their own family members.

3. The student will know what is meant by job families as stated in the scope and sequence.

4. The student will be able to identify aesthetic and material values of careers.

5. The student will be able to identify certain tools related to careers.

6. Student will be able to name a career that involves a group of people and list the requirements needed to make this group operate effectively.

7. Student will be able to name a career that involves the individual and list the requirements needed to make him operate effectively.

8. The student will demonstrate that he has a knowledge of the relationship between the curriculum and career program. (15:7)

The other example appears in "Career Development Guide for the Elementary School," a publication of the State of Maine Department of Education, Bureau of Vocational and Adult Education. The objectives are stated for career development through social studies in grades 1–3:

SOCIAL STUDIES

Rationale

To provide each child an opportunity to form positive values about himself and an introduction to the work world.

General Objectives

Encourage each child to:

1. build a positive attitude toward a larger number of careers.

2. realize the importance of making judgements and decisions in school and the carryover to the world of work.

3. develop a sense of personal worth and self respect.

4. instill a sense of pride in personal and group accomplishments.

5. use the families of class members and other local people to demonstrate different jobs in the classroom.

Performance Objectives

1. To identify and understand the work his father and other family members do.

2. To identify positive attitudes toward careers.

3. To compose rules of conduct and apply these rules to his school situation.

4. To demonstrate that he can contribute to group accomplishments.

5. To describe, through discussion, a broader knowledge of the subject area and how it relates to the world of work. (13:13)

Other Factors of Achieving Program Success

Community involvement is a basic require-ment for program success. Establishing an organization for promoting com-munity-school relationships and for accomplishing the work of developing and implementing careers education is necessary to achieving success. The importance of developing guidelines for directing community members and school personnel in their efforts to bring relevant education to all children cannot be overemphasized. The joint effort of community and school to develop statements of goals and objectives is most significant in the long-range success of the program. How these initial steps are faced and accom-plished will greatly influence continued interest and support for the program, but there are other ongoing activities that also contribute to program success and failure. These other factors are primarily the responsi-bility of the school staff.

The first of these is the development of curriculum. Community members may join in curriculum development activities, but the responsibility for curricular organization rests with the school staff. Determining the nature and needs of children and society can be a joint responsibility, but organiz-ing those needs into a form that facilitates their classroom implementation is left to educators.

A second factor to be met by school people is the analysis of the existing educational program to determine the changes and additions needed to meet the goals and objectives of the new program. In addition to the curricular changes already mentioned, the analysis should reveal new staffing patterns and assignments of present staff, and new staff positions required to meet instructional and leadership demands. The examination should inventory existing materials and equipment and itemize the addi-tions required for careers education. An evaluation of the physical plant and a statement of recommendations for remodeling and for new facilities should be a part of the analysis.

Providing for the continuous evaluation of the program is a third factor of achieving program success. The design, implementation, and continuous program improvement are the responsibilities of district employees. This includes day-to-day and activity-to-activity evaluation by the teacher and children of progress toward program, individual, and personal goals. Feed-back systems that provide evaluative data from all pertinent sources, par-ents, community, administration, teachers, children, etc., must also be established as part of the evaluation process.

A final, all inclusive, factor of success is the day-to-day performance of the instructional staff and the supportive performance of all nonclassroom staff members. Success will be achieved only when all professional educators perform their tasks with the same level of excellence that is the goal of children's performance. When teachers and other educational workers set a model of performance commensurate with the school's expectations for young learners, careers education will be a successful educational program.

Whether careers education ever reaches its full potential as a program capable of putting it all together for education depends on how carefully and completely its shepherds do their work. The success or demise of the program depends on people and their commitment to children and their education.

REFERENCES

1. Buchanan, M. Marcia. "Preparing Teachers to Be Persons." *Phi Delta Kappan,* June 1971, pp. 614–16.

2. Gardner, John W. *Self-Renewal: The Individual and the Innovative Society.* New York: Harper and Row, 1964.

3. Goldhammer, Robert. *Clinical Supervision: Special Methods for the Supervision of Teachers.* New York: Holt, Rinehart and Winston, 1969.

4. Jacobs, Leland B. "Humanism In Teaching Reading." *Phi Delta Kappan*, April 1971, pp. 464–67.

5. Katz, Michael B. *Class, Bureaucracy, and Schools.* New York: Praeger, 1971.

6. Leiberman, Myron. *Education as a Profession.* Englewood Cliffs: Prentice-Hall, 1956.

7. Misner, Paul J., Frederick W. Schneider, and Lowell G. Keith. *Elementary School Administration.* Columbus, Ohio: Charles E. Merrill, 1963.

8. Silberman, Charles E. *Crisis in the Classroom: The Remaking of American Education.* New York: Random House, 1970.

9. Mississippi State Department of Education. *Career Education: A Handbook for Program Initiation.* Jackson: State Department of Education, 1972.

10. Olympus Research Corporation. *Career Education: A Handbook for Implementation.* Salt Lake City: Olympus Research Corporation. Baltimore: Maryland State Department of Education, 1972.

11. Pleasant Hill School District. "Teacher Guide for Increasing the Vocational Awareness of Elementary School Children." Pleasant Hill, Oregon: The District, August 1971.

12. School District of the City of Pontiac. "Annual Report Career Development Program." Pontiac, Michigan: The Project, 1971.

13. State of Maine, Department of Education, Bureau of Vocational and Adult Education. "Career Development Guide for the Elementary Schools." Augusta: The Department, (no date given).

14. State of Nebraska, Department of Education. "Career Education: A Position Paper." Lincoln: Department of Education, 1972.

15. Tigard School District. "Tigard Career Education Program." Tigard, Oregon: The District, 1972.

16. West Virginia Department of Education. "A Guide for the Development of Career Education." Charleston, West Virginia: The Department, June 1972.

Chapter 6 PUTTING IT ALL TOGETHER

Introduction

Education should make a difference. It should make a difference in what individuals find in life and what they contribute to the lives of others. Silberman says: ". . . education should prepare people not just to earn a living but to live a life—a creative, humane and sensitive life" (9:114). Education should help each human to anticipate every day with the hope for happiness and fulfillment that is the reward for personal achievement, positive human relationships, and service to others. An outcome of education should be the ability to seek, enjoy, and improve the "good life," and realization of this objective should begin upon entering the elementary school.

Through the process of guiding individuals toward personal fulfillment, education should help people become aware of one another's needs and desires and, consequently, become concerned about the happiness and welfare of others. Survival will depend, not upon more technological advancements, but upon how each of us manifests our concern for others through our behavior. Education must be a humanizing process that results in a willingness to adjust our way of life so as not to deny life or the requirements of living to others. Education should have as an objective the reduction of "man's inhumanity to man."

For many children, the value system they acquire prior to embarking upon their formal education (and too often the value system they find being rewarded in educational institutions) is contrary to the value system that is basic to humanistic behavior. Belok, et al., in discussing the process of value acquisition, describe the values that seem to be rewarded in our culture.

> Thus he learns that disobedience is bad and obedience is good. He learns to place the highest value on making money; that cheating on tests is clever; that crime is in getting caught; that learning a lot of words is getting an education; that teamwork is preferable to individual effort; that the fellow who is different is bad; that he should not examine what has been labeled evil; that he shouldn't get involved; to avoid issues that are uncomfortable; that we are the good ones; that sex is bad; to always look on the bright side—don't be a kill-joy; to have fun; to associate with the right kind of people; that justice always triumphs; that if things go wrong, the fault lies with the stars; that one never starts a fight, but if he hits you, hit him back; that you can "tell" a person by the street he lives on or where he buys his clothing; that our generalizations about values must be regarded as certainties, regardless of the fact that conflicting value systems can be found all over the globe; that wars must be fought as a method of settling differences when everything else fails. (2:8)

The teachers of this nation's young are the most important people in the world today because of the relationship between learning and behavior, and the need to achieve humanistic goals. Upon their shoulders rests the awesome responsibility of instilling the desire and the means for survival in future generations of Americans. A concurrent and more important responsibility goes beyond mere physical survival and considers the quality of human existence. It is completely inconceivable to promote the conditions of human survival and not promote the conditions of human relationship that will result in more awareness and consideration for our fellow humans than appears to exist today. Elementary schools should direct their energies to this end.

In order to make decisions about the appropriate direction for elementary education to take, it is necessary to have an understanding of the potential of the education of the young in our society. John I. Goodlad, and those associates who helped in the preparation of *Behind the Classroom Door,* listed six values of childhood schooling that provide an excellent base from which to initiate proposals for change in educational programs of young learners and is an excellent reference to ensure continuity of direction.

> *We believe that the best hope for a self-renewing society is a self-renewing individual who has been provided with every possible opportunity to develop his unique talents and capabilities.*

We believe that the development of rational powers is the good work for which education is admirably suited and uniquely responsible.

The educated man is fully aware of societal restraints, the reasons for them, and their appropriateness or inappropriateness for mankind.

The most useful learning is to have learned how to learn.

Education is a life long process in which schooling plays a decreasingly significant role.

There are many roads to learning. (5:9–11)

One means of overcoming the confusion and lack of agreement over the purposes of elementary education is to seek an organizing concept around which all educational programs can be unified and within which educators can find satisfaction for their individual concerns. It is not possible for careers education to be all things to all people, but it is possible for it to serve as a central theme to a program that strives for academic excellence, social sophistication, civic responsibility, and vocational competence.

The intent of elementary school careers education should prevent it from becoming "just another educational fad." Careers education seeks to do what education has always intended to do. It intends to employ societal expectations as a prime criterion for judging the worth of all aspects of school learning and to focus planning of learning experiences on the needs of individuals. Its intent includes equipping learners with the attitudes and skills needed to ensure the survival of our nation and our democratic way of life. Educators who advocate the careers approach believe that its chances for survival and for accomplishing these goals are better than some of the already tried and failed approaches for a number of reasons. Among these reasons are:

1. Careers education is organized to meet the needs of both present and future living of learners rather than on content and experiences that are remote from the real world of children. It is based on the premise that learning is enhanced by actively involving learners in those experiences that are of educational concern to the realization of immediate self-fulfillment in the life roles. It is believed, for these reasons, that children will find relevance in the program and, consequently, give their needed support to it.

2. In careers education, subject matter is not seen as an end in itself but as a means of making more lasting those attitudes, skills, and knowledge that assist individuals in making appropriate life decisions and participating in the processes of social and political interaction.

3. Elementary school careers education reduces the inhibiting confusion that frequently pervades curriculum activity by providing administrators, curriculum specialists, and teachers with an

understandable theme around which they can organize the school program and from which they can launch efforts to provide continuity to the learning experiences of children. It should help eliminate the foggy understanding that often prevents educational change and improvement.

4. The careers approach is capable of being explained, understood, and defended to the public. It should help to resolve many of the problems of communication that exist between parents, taxpayers, and educators, and unite them in a common effort directed at providing the young with the best possible learning opportunities and conditions. This should be a major step in regaining confidence in public education.

5. Elementary school careers education attempts to give new meaning and importance to those educational practices that have been proven sound and successful ways of helping children learn. The idea that everything "old" must be replaced by something "new" is not part of the philosophical base of the program. It is believed, however, that only those educational practices that give meaning to the processes of humanization are worthy of salvation and that new alternatives must meet the "capacitation" criteria if they are to be exposed to children. Elementary school careers education intends to take full advantage of what is known about children, learning, and instruction, and to accept responsibility for advancing that knowledge.

The *mission* of elementary school careers education is the establishment of educational conditions that permit and encourage individuals to become capacitated. The *products* of elementary school careers education are capacitated individuals who have a personal sense of fulfillment and adequacy and who see themselves and others as, "able rather than unable, friendly rather than unfriendly, worthy rather than unworthy, internally rather than externally motivated, dependable rather than undependable, and helpful rather than hindering" (3:12–13). Such people, regardless of their socioeconomic position, contribute to the improvement of the quality of living for themselves and those immediately about them and are productive participants in advancing human conditions for people of all races, creeds, and occupations.

Elementary school careers education is built around the theory that living and learning are not mutually exclusive and that neither is a fragmented experience. It emphasizes those areas of living that: (1) determine the happiness of the child, (2) are of greatest concern to parents, (3) give positive direction to educators, and (4) cause the greatest problems in the community if neglected. Further, the experiences of living are, in the main, focused upon the individual's role as a family member, as a citizen, as a member of a vocation, and as a pursuer of avocational interests and that learning is the means of achieving personal and societal goals in these life careers. Further, it is held that the product of elementary education should be a positive self-concept, skill in human relations, intellectual power, and the acquisition of knowledge. It is also believed that aesthetics and spiritual and moral values permeate all aspects of living and learning and are the binding agents that provide a basis for consistent decision making in a world that is not always consistent.

The emphasis on family membership, citizenship, and vocational and avocational selection is not an attempt to provide a narrowly conceived curriculum. It is an attempt to set a new frame of reference for children. It provides a wide variety of new experiences through which children can develop the habits of thinking and questioning in terms of life roles that will help them answer their "now" questions as they develop patterns of behavior appropriate to seeking humane direction in their adult lives. It is intended that careers education equip elementary school children with the knowledge, skills, and attitudes necessary for making effective and personally rewarding decisions at the proper time rather than expecting them to make specific vocational and avocational selections, determine what their families' present and future should be, or focus upon a single model of citizenship behavior.

School and Classroom Organization

One of the current problems in education is that there is little or no relationship between the learning experiences outside the school in the immediate lives of youngsters and in their later years. The fragmented, diffused approach employed in organizing content and learning experiences in numerous schools has no counterpart in the lives of individuals who have realized success in solving the problems and making the decisions that have resulted in self-fulfillment. Schools need to become a part of society by ensuring that those life roles that determine individual fulfillment also contribute to the fulfillment of children in the school setting. It is easy to accept the fact that children have careers as family members and as citizens, and it should not be difficult to accept the possibility of their having learning experiences closely parallel to participation in vocational and avocational careers. It is to this end that schools in which careers education has been adopted are directing their organizational efforts.

It is necessary that education has an immediate importance to children. Learning must hold a "now" significance and they must have many opportunities to use what has been learned in coping with the matters of their young lives, if learning is to become their permanent possession. Elementary school careers education *is* a here and now way of living in the elementary classroom and school. The total school and each classroom should be a community in which there are citizens, vocations, and avocations, and from which children return to families with an understanding of that unit of society in which they can test and experiment with values and after these values have been sorted through their intellectual processes, they can be internalized as personal guides to decision making and serve as a basis for developing positive human relations.

The classroom and the school must be a "real" environment in which real people make decisions and solve problems that concern their own welfare and the welfare of their peers. The problems they face must be related to the goals they seek with appropriate solutions improving the quality of school living. Inappropriate solutions and decisions need not reduce the quality of living but should provide opportunities for children to learn to face their mistakes and lower their fear of failure. They are also provided opportunities to face the consequences of their decisions in an environment that will not destroy them. The environment must encourage successful living.

Maximum development in all careers requires that children be involved in the processes and the experiences of determining the quality and establishing the conditions of school and classroom living. They should have a voice in defining the learning environment and share in the responsibility for creating it. They should be included in the processes of setting the immediate goals of learning and in prescribing the individual and group behavior that is most complimentary to goal achievement. They should be helped in the identification of their own weaknesses, the evaluation of their own progress, and the assessment of their own organizing efforts.

Functional democratic knowledge and skills and lasting democratic attitudes and appreciations can be developed only in situations that are truly democratic. Discovering that there is no freedom in the absence of rules and order does not occur when rules and order are set through dictatorial one-way communications. Discovery results from participation and need. When schools and classrooms are organized as working models of American democracy, children are more inclined to discover both the need for order and the human relationship skills required to establish it. Under these conditions, they learn the self-control that is basic to freedom. Weber and Weber state that children learn this in their play and that

Living is also a game. We may warm up and spar so to speak, but real
living does not begin until we apply the rules and regulations of the social
milieu which govern our contacts with those with whom we are to live.
(12:4)

Every American institution, school, business, industry, the home, the
churches, and others, if democracy is to succeed, must give people opportunities to grow continuously in their abilities to foresee consequences, to
develop basic principles, to forumulate policies, and to make decisions.
... It is more vital that people be taught how to assume more and more
responsibility in control by consensus than it is to teach them any body
of knowledge. ... The skill of participation in control is more important
than any other skill in American life. Without such skill, the very foundation of democracy cannot stand. (12:11–12)

The principles of democracy are not always easy to foster in the schools
and classroom, for democracy demands that the people determine the kind
of life they want and the form of controls that will ensure it. The goal for
young children is to learn the principles. They are not expected to have
mastered them. The processes of learning require time, patience, and persis-
tence, and will not reach fruition when teachers prefer the easier dictatorial
methods, or when school organization belies the basic tenets of America.

Curriculum Organization

The infusion of elementary school careers edu-
cation into an on-going program should not necessarily destroy the existing
curriculum if it was developed by the staff in a professionally competent
manner. If the existing curriculum is meeting successfully its obligations to
the achievement of educational objectives, the addition of careers education
should enhance rather than hinder continued success. If on the other hand,
the existing curriculum is in need of revision or replacement, there cannot
be a better vehicle for change than careers education.

It is recommended that consideration be given to adopting a spiral curricular organization. The concept of spiral development assumes that learning occurs most effectively when concepts are re-encountered at
ever-increasing levels of complexity and that the thought processes develop
in logical order. The late Hilda Taba described spiral concept development
in the following way:

The hierarchical nature of the concepts makes it impossible to develop
them fully in one unit or even in any one grade level; they must be dealt
with in several grade levels. The concepts must be visualized as threads
which appear over and over again in a spiral fashion but which always are
moving to a higher level. (10:14)

Regardless of whether general curricular rebuilding is to take place, careers education should be integrated with the "spiral" in mind.

In most programs, careers awareness has been designated that part of career development assigned to the elementary school; exploration has been relegated to the middle or junior high school years and the senior high school; and post-secondary education has been charged with the responsibility for developing career specialization. How ideal it would be if learning could be that neatly packaged! Awareness is a life-long learning experience as in exploration and specialization or preparation. Instructional avoidance of any one of these areas at any level will not make it disappear. The answer is a curriculum that takes advantage of reality and provides for content and experiences that will ensure an ability to understand and apply the learning resident in the program.

The answer to the question, "What is career awareness?" was given in *CAPES,* a booklet published by the office of the Washington State Superintendent of Public Instruction.

> Career awareness describes that part of the career education program designed for the elementary grades, K–6. Specifically, the objectives of the K–6 career awareness program are to:
>
> > develop in each student positive attitudes about the personal and social significance of work
> >
> > develop each pupil's self-awareness
> >
> > develop and expand the pupils knowledge about a wide variety of occupations
> >
> > assist students in developing their career aspirations
> >
> > improve overall student performance in the basic subjects by relating them around a career development theme. (11:7)

These are worthy objectives that are most appropriate for inclusion in an elementary school careers education program, or a junior high school program, or a senior high school program—and beyond. Work attitudes, self-concept, occupational knowledge, career aspirations, and basic skills should not be denied complete development by limiting the curricular assignment to only one level. Careers education, like all learning, is a birth to death experience and the public school portion of it must be organized in a continuous K–12 program that provides opportunities for students to become increasingly sophisticated in the understanding of knowledge, in the processes of thinking, and in skill performance.

No clear-cut line of definition exists between careers awareness and careers exploration. Careers exploration, like careers awareness, is an on-going process that begins early and should cease only with death. Exploratory activities can be identified readily as young children assume various career roles in their daily play. It is the responsibility of working adults to be exploring constantly for new and better ways of performing in all the careers and for new opportunities or new careers in their vocational and avocational worlds. This is a requirement in a rapidly changing technological society.

Specialization and preparation for careers begin with the early activities and experiences of children. Individual interests and abilities are often ignored in both home and school but if the individuality of young humans could become a significant consideration in the construction of curricula, career specializations and preparation would meet the objective of students learning job-entry skills before they leave the upper levels of public education with considerably less frustration than is now experienced.

It is possible to give extra emphasis to certain learning areas at different age levels of children, but this must be built carefully into the program in a way that precludes any chance of overemphasis of the identified area or de-emphasis of other areas. The identification of areas of emphasis must be accomplished on the basic needs of learners and program objectives, not on the basis of private interests of the staff. Thus, awareness, exploration, and preparation can be successfully given a varying degree of importance at different levels within the structure of a spiral curriculum.

The Role of Subject Matter

The outcomes of education should have some permanence in the lives of learners. They should contribute continuously to achieving life's goals rather than merely solving for children the immediate problems of getting good marks and pleasing adults. But where does the permanence come from? Does the mastery of subject matter satisfy the permanence criterion? If not, what is the role of subject matter in acquiring permanent benefits from the educational experience? How does all of this translate into the intent and purpose of career education?

Those who condemn subject-centered curricula and outcomes of learnings based on the accumulation of facts often attempt to leave the impression that there is no place for subject matter in humanistically conceived instructional programs. In truth, there is no instructional program where there is no subject matter. Subject matter is not the whole body but it is the organ that supplies the blood for learning to any soundly designed educational effort. There is nothing professionally disreputable in being concerned about content and its value, how it can be best organized for instruction, and what is the most effective method of employing it to bring about positive and permanent change in the behavior of children. The difficulty arises when subject matter is equated with facts.

Subject matter defined as a collection of facts will have only fleeting importance to children, if it has any importance at all. Facts are transient and an instructional approach based only upon their accumulation will do little more than meet the immediate demands of "keeping school." Subject matter must assume a broader definition that telegraphs its intent in terms of achieving the outcomes of education. Anderson's definition suggests a broader interpretation of the intent of content.

> Subject matter is defined as the principles, techniques, facts, values, processes and modes of response that man has learned about the world in which he lives, himself, and his relationships to his environment. Since it encompasses more than is found in a particular book on a specific subject, the selection of subject matter involves more than the selection of books. (1:466)

Meil, in discussing content, includes subject matter as part of the more comprehensive term and further extends the idea that there is more to education than confronting facts.

> We must include within the term not subject matter alone, but also skills for searching out, organizing and using information and skills for handling various types of symbols, media, and tools. We must include also thought processes such as reasoning and criticizing and both analytical and intuitive approaches to data taken in by the senses. (8:408–9)

In careers education, that content which has been identified by the school as most appropriate to the achievement of educational objectives is not replaced by new content that deals more exclusively with the nature of the various careers. Instead, the transition from conventional programs to careers education programs involves examining existing content for its careers possibilities and supplementing areas of weakness. As teachers accept careers education as the most appropriate means of bringing relevant learning to children, the transition may eventually result in significant changes in content and that content will become more and more appropriate to the objectives of education. It is also believed that the processes of content identification and materials selection will become more efficient and effective as the result of the more understandable nature of careers objectives.

A special note to teachers is appropriate. At times there has been a feeling among teachers and teacher educators that emphasis in the preparation of elementary teachers should be in pedagogic detail rather than in content. No room for argument is found in placing importance on the art and science of teaching but there is room for legitimate concern when content is dealt with only superficially in favor of redundant encounters with stagnant methodologies and "cute" teaching ideas. Those teachers who possess the greatest command of the subject matter they teach should also have the greatest capability of employing it as a vehicle to establish with children the more permanent processes of living and learning. It is not a psychological surprise that when subject matter is used as a means of perfecting the learning of processes, it becomes more permanent than when it is considered an end in itself.

In this same sense, children should be helped to gain more than a passing glimpse of the subject matter of their educational experiences. The development of higher level thought processes demands an in-depth involvement of subject areas. The task of becoming a sophisticated problem solver and decision maker requires that learners come in contact with and understand those processes in relationship with more than shallow content and irrelevant facts. Children should be permitted and encouraged to explore in depth areas of interest that possess more than momentary excitement for them. Attitudes, skills, and knowledge gained through such explorations possess the unique permanence that comes from personal discovery.

Development in the several careers can be most satisfactorily accomplished through subject matter which brings to the learner the facts, terminology, principles, and values most related to the career processes being considered. The subject matter selected must provide also for establishment of relationships among the careers through providing possibilities for transfer of learning. Quality of learning can be related to the number and variety of situations and circumstances to which it can be applied successfully. Subject matter (and instructional strategies) should be selected with this quality of learning in mind.

Emphasizing processes does not alleviate the need to give careful consideration to the selection of subject matter. Subject matter must compliment the nature of the goal to be achieved, even when the goal is a process.

Learning Experiences

Children judge the worth of an educational program in terms of the interest and excitement they experience as beneficiaries of the learning activities of the program. The support children give to educational programs is directly related to the immediate reaction they have to the learning experiences in which they participate. When children find personally significant and achievable goals available to them, they will join the activity with an enthusiasm characteristic of the adventurous nature of their age.

The success of elementary school careers education is dependent upon learning activities that offer children a sense of purpose, a sense of reality and relevance that has been foreign to a majority of elementary school classrooms. In career education, less time is spent keeping children occu-

pied with "teacher-trivia," and more time is devoted to helping them discover rewarding means of meeting the challenge and solving the problems
of learning. These conditions require that children share in the tasks of
selecting and designing learning activities. If they are excluded, the possibilities that the activities will possess child appeal are greatly reduced. They
need to feel that the program is theirs and no matter how carefully a teacher
selects a learning experience, it will belong to the teacher and not to the
children.

There is no limit to the activities in which children can find personal
identity. Both the school world and the out-of-school world need to be
recognized and unified in the search for ready sources of learning experiences. Some of the more obvious sources of real problems that have immediate importance in the lives of children and from which children can identify
activities are listed below:

1. The nature of the elementary careers education program should be
   a prime source of learning experiences. The problems inherent in
   defining and creating a living environment centered around the
   careers should provide an almost inexhaustible supply of activities
   appropriate for achieving the goals of learning.

2. Providing for individual and group interests should further add to
   the source of experiences. It is expected that such interests will be
   closely related to the careers and will add a factor of personal
   involvement to the activity.

3. Individualizing and personalizing the program will give children
   additional opportunities to identify important activities to be included in their learning activities. It can even be hoped that they
   will become aware of the individuality of classmates and make
   provisions and adjustments for uniqueness as they select activities.

4. Obviously, teachers should be a ready source of ideas for children.
   Teachers should be available to children who are seeking sugges-
   tions rather than place themselves in a position of being the only
   acceptable source of learning experiences.

5. The stated curriculum of the school should at least offer some
   learning alternatives. It should not dictate the total program but
   should serve as a guide to ensure movement toward major objectives. Children should have an awareness of the intent of the school
   program as reflected in the curriculum. This is a source of learning
   experiences that involves learners in the more formal aspects of
   education.

6. The community—the world beyond the school—must become an
   important extension of the careers program and be researched care-

fully by both teachers and children for: (a) problems worthy of their attention, (b) issues that citizens should not avoid, (c) opportunities to relate school to community and community to school, and (d) human resources that can assist children in the solution of their problems and aid in their learning about the human factors of quality living.

It is not irresponsible professional behavior to involve children in identifying and implementing the experiences of their own learning. The processes required are basic to problem solving on all levels for problems must be identified and the means of solution must be implemented before resolution can occur. Not only does this kind of involvement give children a feeling of personal attachment to their school, it also provides an opportunity for them to internalize a process that will have increasing importance to them.

The inclusion of children in the process of identifying and designing their own learning experiences adds to rather than reduces the teacher's responsibilities for making every school experience a beneficial one. Their task becomes one of taking full instructional advantage of each activity selected by children by searching out "teachable moments" to advance all aspects of learning. The basic skills are introduced, perfected, and given meaning at every opportunity in which there is a need for a basic skill in resolving the problem that made the activity acceptable and interesting to children. It is the teacher's responsibility to identify and, when possible within the parameters of the problem, create opportunities for children to re-encounter previous learnings at increasing levels of complexity and sophistication. This approach requires that teachers make available subject matter that contributes to both the immediate activity and to the total accumulation of knowledge. Teachers need to ferret from these group-selected activities opportunities to identify individual needs and instructional openings for meeting them. Planning and evaluating are continuous teacher activities that should, in addition to keeping children constantly aware of their careers growth and achievement, keep teachers alerted to how exhaustively they have searched each activity for possible learning opportunities.

The teaching model employed in implementing child-selected activities places special emphasis on those instructional responsibilities that precede and succeed teaching performance in the presence of children. The thoroughness of planning and preparing for active teaching and the objectivity of reflection and evaluation following the teaching act crucially influences the quality of instruction. Securing maximum careers education advantage of accepted experiences and activities makes it essential that teachers create an instructional cycle that includes *instructional pre-activities, instructional activities,* and *instructional post-activities.*

Teachers are not uninvolved bystanders to the process of selecting and implementing learning experiences nor does the process permit children "to do as they desire." The nature of the process requires that teachers be involved and their involvement provides the direction and guidance children need to find meaningful activities. Learning to set goals, identifying and defining the problems associated with achieving goals, designing and implementing activities required in solving the problems, and determining when the goals have been reached are highly complex developmental learning experiences basic to the process of selecting learning activities. To become competent in these areas requires that children receive maximum quality instruction over an extended period of time. If the instructional efforts of the teachers are successful, the appropriateness and significance of the activities selected will continually improve and if teachers guide children toward career-oriented experiences, their ability to solve problems will reflect in how they perform the life roles.

It is not intended that all learning experiences should be identified by children. They should be included in the activities of selection in terms of their ability to contribute effectively to the process. This means that, if teachers are successful, children should become increasingly involved in their own learning as they advance through school. This places at least three identifiable responsibilities on teachers: (1) they must teach children the processes of problem solving and decision making; (2) they must permit children to exercise their problem-solving and decision-making skills on behalf of their own learning; and (3) they must attempt to make teacher-selected activities fit the pattern of their children's interests and immediate concerns.

Whether or not an activity or a problem identified by children becomes a viable learning experience depends upon what the teacher does or perhaps does not do after young learners have agreed that their selection is deserving of their time and effort. Establishing the processes to be followed in solving the problem removes teachers from the roles of prescribers, ultimate authorities, and givers of answers and places them in the roles of guides, resource persons, and questioners. These teacher roles are not discrete. Guiding takes the form of helping children discover alternative routes to their goals. This is done by performing the roles of resource person and questioner. A significant and carefully timed piece of new information or a question can ignite new thought processes that will guide children to additional alternatives and perhaps more appropriate means of problem solution. Only through a process of guided discovery can children become independent decision makers and meet this major goal of careers education.

The difference between being able to take this kind of advantage of learning activities selected by children and not being able to do so is the difference between being a professional educator and being an educational technician.

Use of Community Resources

Careers education is community-centered education. The relevancy criterion of elementary careers education makes it necessary for children to find relationships between the career experiences they have in school and career experiences outside the school. This requires the expansion of the school into the community and the inclusion of many community members and activities in the program of the school. The manner in which the school and the community are brought together in this educational enterprise determines the learning benefits to be gained by children.

One of the few attempts that has been made to bring the school and community together in a careers education fashion has been the study of "community helpers" during the early elementary years. This activity has taken many forms over the years but most often it has been restricted to reading information presented in basic texts. Teachers occasionally have invited workers from the community into the classroom to talk about their specific occupations and to answer children's questions. Seldom has the guest list included a wide range of occupations and it usually has been limited to employees of tax-supported services. These experiences may have been or may continue to be initiated as a result of careful educational thought and planning but they fall far short of meeting the requirements of careers education.

The involvement of "workers" in the career experiences of children should be focused on promoting "helping relationships" rather than be a situation in which they "tell" about themselves. Resource people from the community should be invited into the classroom only when activities require the help of a specialist or a service that can be provided best by someone outside the school. Children need to experience personal involvement in situations where the vocational skills and human competencies of a variety of "workers" contribute to the solution of problems that are important to the class. Children should not be involved in activities in which guests in the classroom are placed at a disadvantage or in which they are forced to judge the worth and dignity of an occupation on the verbal sophistication and cleverness of one of its practitioners. Guests should be accepted in terms of the contribution they and their specialty can make to solving learning problems.

Tours into the community by children should take place because the problem at hand requires community assistance in its solution; not because the third grade has always gone to the ice cream plant or because there is extra room on the bus being used by another group. The community should be made an integral part of the learning arena by giving each field trip a purpose that is related to a learning activity. This could mean confronting issues where they occur, exploring situations that do not exist in the school, questioning people whose answers can be arrived at only in the community, observing an operation that has no classroom equivalent, or applying classroom learning to a community situation.

The relationship between community members and children on field trips should be similar to those expected when people from the community join children in the classroom. There must be some assurance that both leave the scene with a feeling of closeness and understanding for each other that may not have existed previously. Children should come away from the experience with a better understanding and appreciation for the contribution community workers make to their lives. They should re-enter the school with a clearer view of human interdependency and career interrelationships. Evidence should indicate that each contact with the community will do this for children before it is included in the educational program.

Work Attitudes

It may appear illogical to discuss work attitudes at this point rather than under the "Vocational Career" in chapter 3. It is done in an attempt to: (1) exemplify the ubiquitous nature of attitudes and that consideration of the development of any attitude should not be restricted to one career, (2) dispel any idea that careers education is "vocational education," and (3) demonstrate that all elementary careers educational experiences should be designed to take advantage of all possible opportunities to develop threads of relationships among the careers.

Attitudes and values have been one of the most perplexing instructional problems in public education for a long time. The personal nature of attitudes and the processes of internalizing values along with a lack of understanding of their acquisition have caused this aspect of teaching to be ignored generally. Elementary school careers education may offer some assistance in overcoming these difficulties by helping children make personal value decisions in the atmosphere of the "real" living environment of a careers-oriented program.

Part of the here and now benefits of elementary school careers education should be derived from its concern for revitalizing and making current the work ethic upon which this nation was founded and in the development of related work attitudes. The idea that hard work and a life lived sparingly is good in the eyes of God, and that success is best measured in the accumulation of material goods may not have the same acceptance or importance it once had; but the idea of productive work as a necessary ingredient of living has lost neither its acceptability nor its importance. In this regard, one of the goals of elementary school careers education is to give new emphasis and importance to the attitudes associated with the service aspect of work. This is not to deny nor diminish the dignity of the producer of goods; rather it is to give dignity to the renderer of services and to suggest that goods need to be produced with service to humans in mind.

In the development of work-related attitudes, children in the elementary school must discover dignity in all work that serves the group. This requires that the school and each subgroup within the school be a self-organized society in which a variety of work must be performed in order to meet societal goals. It also requires that children have an opportunity to engage in work from the most menial to the most prestigious and that they be rewarded in terms of performance and not in terms of the nature of the task. The nature of the reward should contribute to the understanding of all concerned that achievement of group goals is dependent upon the work of each member, as well as encourage children to think in terms of service and job happiness rather than social and economic rewards. They should come to understand that human acceptance or rejection is not based on individual or family occupation. If children accept as dignified all work that contributes to the good of society, they should be more inclined to accept all humans as worthy regardless of their occupations.

Children should discover that the achievement of goals, both societal and personal, is dependent upon the quality of the work done by each individual and that excellence of performance has both intrinsic and extrinsic rewards. They should be helped to develop those skills of self-evaluation necessary to arrive at an objective understanding of their potential so that being dissatisfied with less than an excellent performance becomes a way of life. This is not to imply that children should become perfectionists but that they should perform at a level equal to their maximum rather than their minimum abilities. Learners should be made aware that excellence of performance is not limited to the vocational career but that it is equally important to fulfillment in all careers.

"Excellence" is used here to describe a level of performance that is commensurate with an individual's greatest capacity to perform. It is understood that each child will not perform equally in all endeavors but they should be expected to match their efforts with their abilities in each activity in which they participate. In addition, it must be kept in mind that there are many kinds of excellence. John Gardner states:

> In the intellectual field alone there are many kinds of excellence. . . .
> And there is excellence in art, in craftsmanship, in human relations, in
> technical work, in leadership, in parental responsibilities.

> Some kinds of excellence can be fostered by the educational system, and others can be fostered outside the educational system. . . . There are types of excellence that involve doing something well and types that involve being a certain kind of person. There are kinds of excellence so subjective that the world cannot even observe much less apprise them. (4:152)

Another aspect of excellence of performance is identified by Margaret Mead in her discussion of the dichotomy that exists between those who enjoy what they do and those who do not. She suggests that those who are competent and perform at a high level do not distinguish between work and leisure—to them these are one and the same.

> Some prophets are predicting that professional people and people who are technically competent, people who are gifted, will cease to make any distinction between work and leisure, or work and recreation, because for such people, there is no distinction. If they are doing what they want to and enjoying what they are doing, they just have life, that's all. They don't have recreation and they don't have hobbies and they don't have leisure in the ordinary sense of the word at all, just a piece of time to go into something else. (7:46)

Elementary school careers education provides opportunities for students to acquire Mead's idea of total living through encouraging excellence of performance in all life roles and through helping learners discover what they want to do.

Leonard suggests that in the schools of the future there will be even greater rewards from the pursuit of excellence; from exploiting from every learning experience its maximum benefits.

> The notion that ecstasy is mainly an inward directed experience testifies to our distrust of our own society, of the outer environment we have created for ourselves. Actually, the varieties of ecstasy are limitless. . . . The new educator will seek out the possibilities of delight in every form of learning. . . . Indeed, the skilled pursuit of ecstasy will make the pursuit of excellence, not for the few, but for the many, what it never has been —successful. And yet, make no mistake about it, excellence, as we speak of it today, will be only a by-product of a greater unity, a deeper delight. (6:20–21)

There are other aspects of work performance that are directly related to, or a part of, excellence. The first of these is task completion. Children should at the very least be expected to complete, in terms of their individuality, assigned and personally selected tasks and be permitted the personal satisfaction that accompanies bringing a task to its logical conclusion. Encouragement and appropriate assistance is a part of good teaching but the final extrinsic reward should be associated with completing the activity in an excellent manner. This, of course, requires that the job be worth doing and that it be personally appealing and of immediate importance to the child. Learners cannot be expected to complete tasks at a level of excellence that to them are trivial and irrelevant.

Another work attitude and a difficult one to instruct is job responsibility. Tasks should not only be completed and meet the criteria of excellence, they should be completed at the moment they have the most value and in the form that contributes most to the resolution of the need that prompted the job. The implication is that task performance, regardless of quality, should not lose its maximum efficiency through procrastination or its maximum effectiveness through lack of adherence to the direction dictated by the goal to be achieved. This kind of responsibility is necessary to maximum performance in all areas of endeavor.

The interdependent or division of labor nature of some work involves work attitudes that could be considered a part of job responsibility. Task completion and quality in this type of work depends upon each worker meeting his responsibility at a level of performance that will enhance the final product. There are at least two attitudes that children must develop if they are to achieve success in this type of work. The first is the attitude of democratic responsibility. The understanding to be gained here is that democracy involves both rights and responsibilities and that in order to enjoy the results of the work, each participant must fully meet his responsibility to the other participants and to the task. The second attitude is concerned with "self." Each child must be helped to understand that he is a worthy member of the group and that his contribution is important to the successful completion of the task. In order for this to occur, the teacher must see to it that each child does in fact have an important contribution to make to the success of the project and that the contribution is important to the child and within his capabilities.

The development of work attitudes should help children gain an honest feeling of pride in their achievements. They need to experience joy in accomplishment when they know a product of personal effort is worthy of their capabilities. Once experienced, pride of achievement should motivate individuals to persist in their efforts until each life task is resolved in an excellent manner rather than being satisfied or discouraged with a low quality performance.

Summary

Careers education is a birth to death experience. It is a continuous process. Even though development may proceed at different rates among people and at an unsteady pace within individuals, there should not be gargantuan experiential steps either forward or backward or precipitous learning cliffs to falter on or tumble down. The school-based portion of careers development should fit smoothly into the child's life. It needs to be an articulated kindergarten through grade twelve program, absent of life-wasting overlaps and life-consuming gaps. A school system that permits the existence of elementary, junior high, and senior high school "kingdoms" is not ready philosophically for careers education.

Development in each career must also be a kindergarten through grade twelve effort in which the experiences and activities of each age level provide readiness for the experiences and activities of the next age level. Even though learners, as they move from level to level, experience a shift in instructional emphasis among the careers, they will encounter instruction in all careers at all levels (see figure 6-1). Breaking down the following discussion of careers education into primary and intermediate age levels is intended to give a better view of the program and not to indicate that the program should be fragmented into levels.

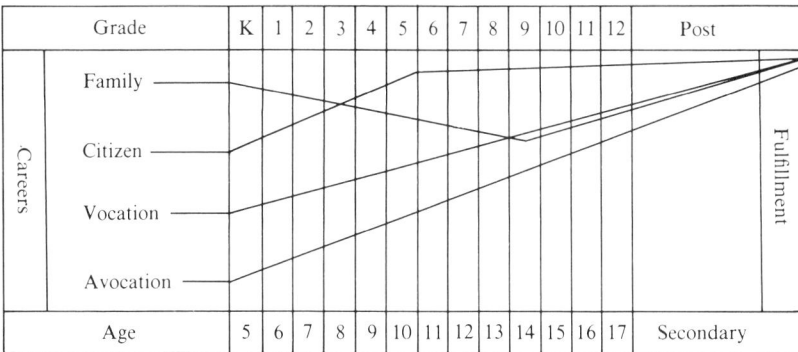

	Grade	K	1	2	3	4	5	6	7	8	9	10	11	12	Post	
Careers	Family															Fulfillment
	Citizen															
	Vocation															
	Avocation															
	Age	5	6	7	8	9	10	11	12	13	14	15	16	17	Secondary	

FIGURE 6-1

RELATIVE INSTRUCTIONAL IMPORTANCE OF EACH CAREER AT EACH
GRADE AND AGE LEVEL

THE PRIMARY LEVEL

The primary school years (K-3 or ages 5-9) are not the beginning as many teachers seem to believe. The beginning occurs at an earlier time and in places so diverse they are indescribable. Children arrive at school very complete human beings in possession of value systems that cause much of the activity of the school to be "reteaching" rather than teaching even though instruction seems to be designed more in keeping with the theory of *tabula rasa*. They have acquired a surprisingly complete set of prejudices and beliefs that influence relationships with others, attitudes toward races and occupations, acceptance of new knowledge, the value of education, the quality of the school, and the worth and dignity of teachers. They have often gained sophisticated command of their native language and an ability to use it effectively to maintain and advance their position in their world. Their development in the cognitive, affective, and psychomotor domains is frequently in advance of the expectations of the school.

The primary level, if not the beginning of living and learning, determines the degree of success children have in many later experiences. It is at this level that children begin to confirm or adjust their attitudes toward school, teachers, and peers. This is the time when a life-long excitement for learning can be established, continued, or destroyed. This is when youngsters learn to accept the easy and deadening way of required conformity or discover the challenge and reward of supported individuality. It is a time in life when creativity can bloom or be buried; and what the child gains or fails to gain during these early years in school will reflect in later performance, not only in school but in later family living, citizenship performance, vocational success, and avocational pursuits.

From a human point of view, the primary years are a time for accepting children as they are and for avoiding giving them negative labels that may last them a life time. This is a time of learning, not a time for giving names to conjectures of why learning cannot occur. Success is the key word in describing the instructional intent of all levels of careers education and particularly for the very young. Success is an internal experience that can be accurately defined only in terms of individuals. The general meaning of success here is that level of performance in all careers experiences needed to promote positive attitudes toward learning and future performance and toward people within and without the school setting, and to enhance self-concept.

From a careers point of view, the primary years are a time for the school to assume its role in helping children find success in developmental processes related to the various careers. The family career and the citizen's career should be given the greatest emphasis during these years. Children in this age group should have experiences that will help them extend and expand their world successfully from the family to the school and that begins for them the processes of becoming aware of the family and of "self" as a family member. These are primarily human relationship experiences designed to help children explore and discover the characteristics of families and family roles and responsibilities.

Primary children should begin to experience those citizenship activities that have to do with establishing their own school living conditions. Activities necessary to accomplishing this are focused on seeking agreement on what classroom environmental conditions are most acceptable to the group and in devising ways of creating them. These are decision-making and problem-solving activities that are, as often as possible, identified by children. Successful completion of the task should result in observable movement toward improving classroom climate.

Teachers need to relate family role and responsibility to citizenship role and responsibility. The best way to develop this continuity is by using the same kinds of individual and group activities in both situations. One major difference between learning experiences in these two careers is in decision making. Children learn to make decisions by making decisions. This they can do as citizens of their school, who have been given responsibility for establishing and maintaining a quality living and learning environment. They can and will make decisions in this area if they are permitted to do so and are not denied the right by adults. Children will have opinions of their family and their relationships to and within the family, but it does not fall within the realm of positive relationships to encourage children to make public decisions relative to the condition of their families. The school's responsibility is to help children see beauty and human goodness in their world. For some children, looking for these qualities in their family is a discouraging experience and for them especially there must be beauty and human goodness in the school.

Even though the vocational and avocational careers are not given primary emphasis at this level, neither are they ignored. The occupational awareness activities that make up the total career education program in a majority of primary programs are appropriate and should be included but they are far less important to vocational career development at this time than is the development of related attitudes and skills. Awareness activities do contribute to attitude and skill development but to limit consideration of the vocational career to one kind of activity would deny children the opportunity to acquire as a way of life the application of positive work attitudes and skills to all endeavors in all careers.

It is important at the primary level to initiate the development of those vocational attitudes that are important throughout life. Attitudes that relate to finding dignity in all socially useful work, craftsmanship, and excellence, job responsibility, task completion, and pride in accomplishment should be made as important to children as they ought to be to adults. What teachers expect of children and how children are rewarded must be in agreement with the nature of the attitudes being developed and teachers must exemplify in their relationships with children and in the work they do, the attitudes that are held to be important outcomes of education.

It is difficult to isolate and discuss specific vocational skills that require special instructional attention in the primary years. All the skills that receive attention at this level have later vocational implications. What is needed is a better distribution of the consideration given and time spent

among the three domains. Admittedly, there is a better balance among the
domains in these early years of school than at any other level, but the
psychomotor development of children needs more attention than it now
receives. More effort needs to be directed toward developing physical coordination in the use and manipulation of equipment and tools. The skills
associated with being physically effective and efficient, as well as the attitudes basic to keeping physically fit, are a part of this domain that demand
inclusion in the school program.

The nature of affective and cognitive skills requires that they be given
equal attention in the development of young children. These two domains
need to be viewed as closely related areas that cannot be developed sepa-
rately. There is no place in public education for affective development to
compete with cognitive development, social sciences to oppose science, or
humanism to combat technology. The goal is not to fragment society but
rather to help children acquire those skills needed to unify it. The objective
is to assist each individual in gaining the skills and attitudes needed to
advance human conditions and improve the quality of living. The ideal time
to initiate progress toward these goals is at the primary age.

Avocational activities that hold special individual meaning and reward
are needed by children for the same reasons they are needed by adults.
Many children need the diversity of experience and the balance of activity
that can come from a program that offers avocational alternatives to them.
These choices will add an important dimension to all careers and provide
opportunities for children to explore a variety of avocational possibilities.
Hopefully, these activities will carry over from school to home and community, thus providing one more thread of continunity in the child's life.

THE INTERMEDIATE LEVEL

The intermediate school years (grades 4-6, or ages 9-12) do not begin with
a sudden change in the physical, social, or intellectual nature of the child
as the organization of some schools and the statements of some writers
might suggest. Development is continuous, not always "onward and up-
ward," but in uneven inclines and plateaus that, on an individual basis, are
not distinguishable or identifiable by grade level or chronological age. Intermediate age children should continue to develop those attitudes and skills
and to expand the knowledge that was initiated during the primary years.
The family and citizenship careers should continue to be of greatest concern
with citizenship receiving an increasing emphasis. Citizenship experiences
at this age level are concerned with maintaining the classroom learning and
living conditions established earlier and with adjusting the environment to
accommodate changing peer relationships. More emphasis should be given
to individual citizenship responsibility and performance in an attempt to

help students deal with group pressures. Decision making in this career is directed at helping children find a realistic relationship with schoolmates through analyzing group situations in light of personal values and reacting appropriately. Many opportunities should be provided for students to make and test citizenship decisions and behaviors.

The family career should continue to be emphasized as children in this age group become more aware of themselves and as they begin to feel the pressures of their peer group. Home and the family should provide stability and security in the lives of children who are beginning to enter a time of great social and physical change. For children who come from stable, secure homes, the task of the school is to help them understand, appreciate, and use the family as an intimate environment in which they can explore safely their developing value system. For children who have never experienced life in a secure family or who are experiencing a loss of family security and stability, the school must do so much more.

First, these children must experience stability, security, and warm human relationships in the school. The teacher has a special responsibility to provide these children with an environment in which they feel wanted and to which they feel they belong. Second, they must have in their lives an adult whom they perceive cares about them and who is available to them. An open door policy may be adequate for a school system, but a teacher must have an open arms policy. Third, children should leave the school with an understanding of the importance of the family unit in the lives of its members and in our way of life. Only if they understand the impact that the family has on the present and future success and happiness of its members, will they in their adult lives try to establish and maintain intimate relationships within their families.

All aspects of development in the vocational career should become more specific during the intermediate years. Attitudes related to work should become more mature and more observable in each child. These children should begin to benefit personally from developing work attitudes. They should find personal rewards in completing tasks in a manner commensurate with their ability. A keener awareness of special skills and interests should begin to reflect in individual performance. They should demonstrate more individuality, creativity, and independence in identifying and attacking the work that needs to be done to satisy their own needs and the needs of the group.

Intermediate level children should be guided toward seeing specific relationships between what they are doing to maintain and advance their society and what is being done in the out-of-school world. They should continue to include members of the community in their school activities as a means of increasing their understanding of the world of work. They need to seek opportunities to pursue their skills and interest in the community.

A few children will have made considerable progress toward identifying a specific avocational area of interest. For the majority, the intermediate years will be a time for enjoying many activities and experiences from which individuals might eventually identify an avocation. Avocational activities must continue to be an important part of the school program and children should be encouraged to participate. Recognition must be given for accomplishments in this area as it is in all other areas.

No claim is made that elementary school careers education is the panacea for anything. Like any other program, its success depends upon the people who implement and maintain it. Unlike many innovated programs, it should not be destroyed through the processes of interpretation for its purpose is relevant and its justification is understandable. Learning is seen as the "womb to tomb" means of bringing to humans a happy, productive, and rewarding life. The school is seen as only one location for life's learning to take place.

Whether or not the coat of careers education will be larger, looser, and more practical than that of other contemporary education programs will depend upon how many adult "kingdoms" and vested interests are stuffed into it. If the program is designed exclusively for children, the covering will have that pliability and resiliency characteristic of the growing young. If the goals of the program are to provide interest and excitment in today's learning and relevance and preparation for tomorrow's living, the program's coat will be appropriately nonrestricting.

REFERENCES

1. Anderson, Vernon E. *Principles and Procedures of Curriculum Improvement.* New York: Ronald, 1965.

2. Belok, Michael, O. R. Bontrager, Howard C. Oswalt, Mary S. Morris, and E. A. Erickson. *Approaches to Values in Education.* Dubuque, Iowa: Wm. C. Brown, 1966.

3. Combs, Arthur W., Donald L. Avila, and William W. Purkey. *Helping Relationships: Basic Concepts for the Helping Professions.* Boston: Allyn and Bacon, 1971.

4. Gardner, John. *Excellence: Can We Be Equal and Excellent Too?* New York: Harper and Row, 1961.

5. Goodlad, John I., M. Frances Klein, and Associates. *Behind the Classroom Door.* Worthington, Ohio: Charles A. Jones, 1970.

6. Leonard, George B. *Education and Ecstasy.* New York: Dell, 1968.

7. Mead, Margaret. "The Changing Cultural Patterns of Work and Leisure." In *Education in a Dynamic Society: A Contemporary Sourcebook,* ed. Dorothy Westby-Gibson. Reading, Mass.: Addison-Wesley, 1972.

8. Meil, Alice. "Let Us Develop Children Who Care About Themselves and Others." In *Readings In Curriculum,* ed. Glenn Hass, Kimball Wiles, and Joseph Bondi. Boston: Allyn and Bacon, 1970.

9. Silberman, Charles E. *Crisis in the Classroom: The Remaking of American Education.* New York: Random House, 1970.

10. Taba, Hilda. *Teacher's Handbook for Elementary School Social Studies.* Palo Alto: Addison-Wesley, 1967.

11. Washington State Superintendent of Public Instruction. *CAPES: A Guideline for Career Awareness Programs for the Elementary Schools.* Olympia: Office of the State Superintendent, 1972.

12. Weber, Charles A. and Mary E. Weber. *Fundamentals of Educational Leadership.* New York: Exposition, 1955.

INDEX

137

DATE DUE

JUN 11 '82			
MR 12 '03			

DEMCO 38-297